MBA
In A Week

Alan Finn began his career in the Royal Navy as an engineer in nuclear submarines but now works in B2B marketing and management consultancy for industry, helping usually technological organizations to grow. His MBA – a specialist MBA in strategic marketing from the University of Hull – opened up many more opportunities and allowed Alan to broaden his career and to develop his own consultancy business.

Teach Yourself ®

MBA
In A Week

Alan Finn

First published in Great Britain in 2016 by John Murray Learning. An Hachette UK company.

Copyright © Alan Finn 2016

Published in US by Quercus in 2016

The right of Alan Finn to be identified as the Author of the Work has been asserted by him in accordance with the Copyright, Designs and Patents Act 1988.

Database right: Hodder & Stoughton (makers)

The *Teach Yourself* name is a registered trademark of Hachette UK.

British Library Cataloguing in Publication Data: a catalogue record for this title is available from the British Library.

Library of Congress Catalog Card Number: on file.

Paperback ISBN 978 1 473 60823 8

Ebook ISBN 978 1 473 60822 1

3

The publisher has used its best endeavours to ensure that any website addresses referred to in this book are correct and active at the time of going to press. However, the publisher and the author have no responsibility for the websites and can make no guarantee that a site will remain live or that the content will remain relevant, decent or appropriate.

The publisher has made every effort to mark as such all words which it believes to be trademarks. The publisher should also like to make it clear that the presence of a word in the book, whether marked or unmarked, in no way affects its legal status as a trademark.

Every reasonable effort has been made by the publisher to trace the copyright holders of material in this book. Any errors or omissions should be notified in writing to the publisher, who will endeavour to rectify the situation for any reprints and future editions.

Typeset by Cenveo® Publisher Services.

Printed and bound in Great Britain by CPI Group (UK) Ltd., Croydon, CRO 4YY.

John Murray Learning policy is to use papers that are natural, renewable and recyclable products and made from wood grown in sustainable forests. The logging and manufacturing processes are expected to conform to the environmental regulations of the country of origin.

John Murray Learning
Carmelite House
50 Victoria Embankment
London EC4Y 0DZ
www.hodder.co.uk

Contents

Introduction

This book is aimed principally at aspiring and junior managers, most probably working in offices for large corporations, who want to develop their careers, to get ahead of the crowd and to rise above their peers. They need to learn more broad-based workplace skills across disciplines other than their own but don't have the time or the money to study for a Master of Business Administration (MBA) degree. It may also be useful for those who already have an MBA, earned some years ago, but who want a refresher.

This very practical 'seven-day MBA' does not assume prior knowledge and distils the most practical business insights from MBA studies into easy-to-digest bite-sized chunks. Ambitious people on the corporate ladder see achieving an MBA as a way to get ahead and to demonstrate their ambition – in short, to rise head and shoulders above the ranks of the other junior managers in their organizations.

Creating visions for growth and spearheading their implementation gets you noticed by top management looking for vigorous new blood to lead the organizations of the future. But it is difficult to create all-embracing, organization-wide visions for growth if you don't really understand how the other departments – departments other than yours – work together.

Studies for an MBA degree don't set you apart just because you have a certificate on your office wall. Knowledge of other departments' aims and objectives, and the workplace challenges their managers face, gives you an inside track on how to improve the overall efficiency of the organization – while making sure that your work gets the credit it deserves! The abilities you will develop will gain the respect of your peers, and your own department's increased efficiency will be noticed by senior management.

This seven-day 'MBA In A Week' raises your game – ambitious managers can learn in a week what the experts learn in a lifetime. You will learn how to integrate the objectives and operations of the whole enterprise into new formations that will deliver sustainable growth and increased shareholder value – as well as impress your boss or a potential new employer at interview!

A secondary but important benefit that I hope you will take from this book is self-confidence. Leadership is often demonstrated by a personal aura of understated self-confidence, a sure-footed capability to lead. You will find new abilities that will enable you to take the part of the overall organization for which you have responsibility forward, achieving new business improvements and successes along the way.

That said, it is important to take a disciplined approach when applying the ideas in this book in the workplace. As you read each chapter, make your own personal notes on how you will apply this new knowledge in your part of the business. Remember, too, to answer the multiple-choice questions at the end of each chapter.

Stick with it and measure your growth!

Alan Finn

SUNDAY

Global business pressures and change

This area of business and management studies is fundamental to an understanding of management practice today and its likely paths into the future. It is a foundation on which to build a solid understanding of where the business discipline has been and how it is likely to develop, given today's fundamental societal pressures and the forces now acting upon the world and business.

SUNDAY

MONDAY

TUESDAY

WEDNESDAY

THURSDAY

FRIDAY

SATURDAY

Major pressures

A non-exclusive list of just some of those major pressures, in no particular order, illustrates their effects on world business today. The effects of such changes and new pressures have always driven legislation to govern how organizations are run throughout business history.

- **The world's financial economy** – as we recover from the economic downturn that began in 2007/8 and new legislation is imposed on banks and the international banking system
- **Geopolitical changes** – for example, the emergence of China and India as global powers; Russia's renewed ambitions for geographical expansion in Eastern Europe and the spread of Islamic fundamentalism and conflict in the Middle East
- **Communications** – the increasing power and pervasiveness of computing (e.g. the emergence of the 'Internet of Things' (IoT) and 'big data' and their effects on future patterns of employment)
- **Changes to the nature of security, crime, conflict and policing** – for example, the increasing use of robotics and drones in 'remotely controlled warfare'; the emergence of cyber warfare and cyber espionage; and the rising importance of cyber security
- **The evolution of transportation** – of people, emergency and aid services, raw materials and finished goods...
- **Environmental change** – and its effects on global demographics (e.g. civil-engineering projects in China such as dams and large canals that lead to the relocation of populations and businesses; the retreating ice cap in the Arctic, opening up shorter sea routes and allowing more cost-effective mineral extraction in the region).

Let's look at each of these major pressures in turn.

The world's financial economy

Currently, strengthening growth is seen in the West in the USA and in the UK, although continental Europe still has problems with restructuring to free up trade and business practices and the UK is burdened by national and personal debt. The BRIC countries have seen mixed fortunes in recent years: Brazil has an uncertain future politically; Russia is trying to leverage its mineral wealth while exhibiting territorial ambitions; China struggles with popular demands for more democracy, while a new premier in India is trying to create major change. The picture is even more varied in emerging markets such as Indonesia and Mexico as well as in South American and African countries (the so-called 'Next Eleven').

All this change and uncertainty deters investors and slows up world growth. Investors thrive in conditions of confidence and stability and this is in short supply at present. International banks are facing increasingly restrictive demands on their structures and operations, as many countries, particularly the United States and in Europe, try to ensure that the very negative impact banking crises can have on international economies and trade, as in 2007–14, does not happen again. These underlying conditions form the platform from which businesses must try to grow over the next few years.

Business confidence is directly related to international news on the conditions of the world's major economies and thence to the willingness – or otherwise – of businesses to invest in their futures. Without investment, significant business growth is difficult. For businesses to grow and prosper, overall growth in the outputs of economies as a whole is critical. Economic growth is defined as positive change in the gross domestic product (GDP) of a country over a year and the real economic growth of one country relative to another is an important indicator of business opportunity. GDP must be adjusted for inflation effects over time and the resulting value is called 'real growth'.

Real economic growth leads to major improvements in people's living standards, the expansion of existing markets and the opening up of new markets and opportunities. Thus, economic growth, from increases in GDP, leads to an improved environment for business investment, which then leads to those major improvements in people's living standards, general prosperity and well-being.

According to Valentino Piana, writing in an article published by the Economic Web Institute in 2001, investment plays six macroeconomic roles:

1 It contributes to current demand of capital goods and thus increases domestic expenditure.
2 It enlarges the production base (installed capital), increasing production capacity.
3 It modernizes production processes, improving cost effectiveness.
4 It reduces the labour needs per unit of output, thus potentially producing higher productivity and lower employment.
5 It allows for the production of new and improved products, increasing value added in production.
6 It incorporates international world-class innovations and quality standards, bridging the gap between the more advanced countries and helping exports and an active participation to international trade.

Thus, economic growth is critical to business.

Geopolitical changes

The emergence of China and India as global powers, Russia's new appetite for geographical expansion and the spread of Islamic fundamentalism and conflict in the Middle East are just a few examples of current geopolitical changes that are creating instability in the world today. And, as we have seen previously, change and instability directly affect the climate for investment, economic and business growth.

The *Global Risks 2014* report, issued by the World Economic Forum, highlights 'how global risks are not only interconnected but also have systemic impacts':

'To manage global risks effectively and build resilience against their impacts, better efforts are needed to understand, measure and foresee the evolution

of interdependencies between risks, supplementing traditional risk-management tools with new concepts designed for uncertain environments. If global risks are not effectively addressed, their social, economic and political fallouts could be far-reaching, as exemplified by the continuing impacts of the financial crisis of 2007–2008.'

The World Economic Forum, *Global Risks 2014*, 9th edition

As an example of these interdependencies we need only see how recent changes in energy supplies have affected geopolitical change. The dramatic fall of oil prices in 2014 has had major implications for oil-producing nations not only in the Middle East but also for Russia. This effect – together with sanctions imposed internationally on Russia for its activities in Ukraine – may help to constrain any further geopolitical expansionary ambitions by President Putin and bring stability back to the region.

Communications

There have been major changes in businesses' and individuals' communications in the last three decades, changes largely wrought by technology, most notably the increasing power and pervasiveness of computing. The disruptive (as well as creative) effects of computing and the Internet on industries are shown in the following completely non-exclusive examples:

- global postal systems – owing to the rise of email
- payment systems and banking
- investment, with the increase in crowd-sourcing
- retailing, as consumers' shopping habits change
- entertainment and video rental with the rise of online on-demand providers such as Netflix
- travel, with the arrival of online travel sites and mobile-app-based transportation companies such as Uber

- management and other consultants – making communication and research much easier
- recruitment of people into jobs
- book publishing – self-publishing and the emergence of ebooks
- university teaching – notably, the impact of Massive Open Online Courses (MOOCs).

Technology has also had a broader impact on business and businesspeople:

> *'Business doesn't happen face to face as often as some would like. Instead, today's communication depends on conference calls and emails chains that make it challenging to get to know your partners. It's been a common lament among business people dissatisfied with the technology that has become the norm in their daily lives. But with so many workers worldwide now working in virtual teams, many business relationships do depend on technology. And that's not a bad thing – as long they're using the right technologies in the right ways.'*
>
> Natalie Burg, writing in *ForbesBrandVoice* in October 2013

With instant, global information in their pockets, today's businessmen and businesswomen are never out of touch with information systems or their teams or clients, speeding up business processes incrementally.

Changes to the nature of security, crime, conflict and policing

Examples can be seen readily in the increased use of robotics and drones in remotely controlled warfare but also in traffic and crime policing, personal identity theft, the emergence of cyber warfare and espionage and the increasing importance of cyber-security systems. The potential for disruption that these developments represent should not be underestimated:

'New technologies offer the promise of preventing and mitigating insecurity, but can also enable criminal activity. There is nothing predetermined about these multi-dimensional and multi-level threats to security. To understand how and why potential security threats result in real harm, and what interventions are most likely to improve threat prediction and avoid, reduce and manage risks, is an urgent task for the social sciences. Under the New Security Challenges programme, the ESRC [Economic and Social Research Council] has been examining the changing nature of security and risk, for example funding research on understanding the causes and processes of radicalization and violence in contemporary society.'

Economic and Social Research Council (ESRC), *Strategic Plan, 2009–2014*

The need for policies arising from ESRC's research is obvious and fundamental to securing stable business relationships and trade. Without platforms to address security, business cannot advance as it should and energies, activities and investments will be wasted.

The evolution of transportation

The evolution of the on-time delivery of raw materials and finished goods is a fascinating subject and an area in which great efficiencies can be made to cut costs and increase profits. There are changes taking place in transportation systems:

'Major constraints on global transport demand in the foreseeable future will include energy costs and scarcity, climate change, congestion, urbanization, scarcity of available funding, the ageing population in developed countries and the need to reduce road traffic deaths and injuries. Innovation – including through the application of new technologies, techniques and policies – must play a role in ensuring that transport contributes to a sustainable future.'

Report of the International Transport Forum 2010

But what does all this innovation and change – driven mostly by technology – mean for businesses around the world? Improvements in logistics in a globalizing world have a profound implication for costs – costs of shipping and transport, warehousing of in-bound parts and outbound products – and therefore for profits.

Improving supply chain management

Logistics and supply chain management are major subjects for master's degrees in Business Management. For example, Lancaster University's Business School's Department of Management Science teaches degree courses that have large components focused on the importance and science of data management, one of which is in logistics and supply chain management. This teaches students to use their analytical skills to develop models to improve strategic supply chain management, global sourcing, logistics and 'servitization' – adding value to services as a component.

SUNDAY
MONDAY
TUESDAY
WEDNESDAY
THURSDAY
FRIDAY
SATURDAY

Raw materials and finished goods reqiure transportation to either factories for assembly into final products or to markets to be sold to final customers. This must be done in a timely manner, at a low a cost as possible, to maximize profits, and data can indicate ways to make great efficiencies in supply chains. New ideas for transportation and shipping, ranging from delivery by flying drones to the use of local secure 'lockups', located in places convenient to final customers, right through to shipping by airships or civilian submarines, are all innovative ways of approaching this problem to drive overall transportation costs as low as possible.

Environmental change

Global warming and dramatic global weather effects, including warmer winters and floods in Europe and colder winters in the United States, are impacting business models globally at an accelerating rate, sometimes increasing costs and hitting profits – but sometimes creating new opportunities. For example, the retreating polar ice cap in the Arctic will permit shorter sea routes for transportation as well as allow more cost-effective mineral extraction in the northern polar region.

> *'The new study, GEO-5 for Business, says that the future success of businesses in transport, tourism, finance, food, and other sectors, will hinge on their ability to manage the major risks posed by climate change, depleted natural resources, the loss of biodiversity, and extreme weather conditions. But the study says smart businesses can buck the trend and create competitive advantage, by tapping into future demand for sustainable technologies, services and products, and by reducing their own environmental footprint.'*
>
> Bryan Coll in *The Guardian*, June 2013, reporting on a new study by the United Nations Environment Programme

The key is to spot the opportunities and for investors to support them to balance out the risks inherent in our changing environment. Business success, trade and profits are dependent on many variables, and organizations must take a wide variety of factors into account in their business planning activities, including the environment and climate change. Planning for changed energy demand and utility services are just one set of factors for even the smallest of businesses to take into account in the twenty-first century.

MBA recommended reading list

Janice B. Gordon, *Business Evolution: Creating Growth in a Rapidly Changing World* (CreateSpace, 2014)

Janet Morrison, *The Global Business Environment: Meeting the Challenges*, 3rd edition (Palgrave Macmillan, 2013)

World Economic Forum, *Global Risks*, published annually. This can be downloaded from www.weforum.org/reports/

Summary

The pressures, trends and changes described in this chapter have already affected and will continue to change previous conceptions of how business is carried out and regulated. The changes made to business practices in response to these issues will have an impact on regulation and laws that need to be anticipated by smart businesses to reduce their impact on their bottom lines. Trade associations – groups formed by the management of businesses in discrete areas, from banking to manufacturing, from airlines to mineral miners, that are otherwise competitors – are a useful way to address the big issues faced commonly by businesses in their different sectors. Forecasts of trends can be mutually funded, governments can be lobbied and research supported to address the forces for change that they face together, to get some idea of their shape, size and likely impacts. Knowledge shared in this way reduces businesses' risks and develops pressures to adapt and change business laws.

SUNDAY

MONDAY

TUESDAY

WEDNESDAY

THURSDAY

FRIDAY

SATURDAY

Fact-check (answers at the back)

1. How closely related is daily news on the world economy to general business confidence?
   a) Not at all ❏
   b) Only loosely related ❏
   c) This differs according to geographic areas and economic regions ❏
   d) Daily business news is now dispersed on recipients' preferred social media to great effect ❏

2. How strongly is a positive change in the GDP of one country relative to another an important indicator of business opportunity?
   a) Not a strong indication ❏
   b) Only a very weak signal ❏
   c) This varies totally depending upon counties' different industrial sectors ❏
   d) A very positive signpost ❏

3. Does the emergence of China and India as global powers and an appetite for geographical expansion in Russia have an impact on the stability of the world's economies?
   a) Slightly – only a limited impact ❏
   b) Not at all – global economies are not directly linked to geopolitical tensions ❏
   c) Directly – world stock markets always react negatively to such news ❏
   d) The major effect is locally and on countries with strong trade links to those directly affected ❏

4. How might religious fundamentalism arising in the Middle East affect the world's economies?
   a) No impact at all ❏
   b) Short-term effects die quickly but there are increasingly longer-term results ❏
   c) There is only a limited impact when terrorist attacks occur on, for example, European streets ❏
   d) The Middle East supplies a large amount of oil and gas to world energy markets. Any interruption of supplies by terrorist activities has a large impact on the global economy ❏

5. What impact will the emerging 'Internet of Things' (IoT) have on businesses?
   a) In almost every conceivable aspect of our personal, domestic and business lives ❏
   b) Only to integrate domestic needs and activities, such as the automatic adjustment of heating and cooling systems ❏
   c) Mostly only in terms of logistics and supply chains ❏
   d) This will affect only the smart metering of utility supplies ❏

6. How might 'big data' affect businesses?

a) Since big data shows trends in the take-up of new products, it will affect only advertising ❑

b) By highlighting online shopping habits ❑

c) By exposing aspects for improvement in every area of business as trading moves inexorably to online processes ❑

d) By indicating how to make efficiencies in supply chains and logistics ❑

7. What will be the likely impact of technology on personal and business security systems?

a) Mostly in areas such as drones to control traffic and to attack known terrorists in remote areas of the world ❑

b) Internet snooping may uncover threats to security ❑

c) Cyber security has become a major technological business threat today. It can permit disruption to companies' communications and processes, caused by disgruntled or malicious employees, for which no comprehensive defences are yet in place ❑

d) Technology frequently releases users' confidential information and cannot be controlled ❑

8. How will transport be affected by new innovations?

a) Large civilian submarines may become dominant in carrying cargoes securely by sea and gas-filled airships may fill the skies ❑

b) Fuel costs and engine efficiencies will limit road transport systems ❑

c) Inefficiencies in complex international logistics systems will be exposed by big data, the analysis of which will indicate solutions ❑

d) Road transport is very vulnerable to terrorist activities and will decline ❑

9. Global weather systems are changing – how may they affect trade?

a) Not at all – trade is independent of the weather these days ❑

b) Only trade carried out by means of shipping will be affected ❑

c) All trading activities and supporting systems – from communications with stock markets to energy supplies – are affected ❑

d) Forecasting of global weather conditions will be perfected within a decade ❑

10. Business premises waste a lot of energy. How could businesses respond to this issue?

a) They should ignore variations because energy prices fluctuate so widely anyway ❑

b) Environmentally sustainable energy systems – wind, tidal or solar energy systems – are beginning to provide most of our energy so they should budget for lower costs ❑

c) They should plan for changing energy demands and alternative utility services ❑

d) They should audit premises' energy use and plan to reduce it by insulation, reduced heat loss and investment in more efficient heating and cooling plants ❑

SUNDAY

MONDAY

TUESDAY

WEDNESDAY

THURSDAY

FRIDAY

SATURDAY

MONDAY

Finance, economics and accounting

Finance, economics and accounting are each a different field of study but with similarities and overlaps:

- Finance is the study of how to allocate assets efficiently and is forward-looking, so as to develop an understanding of what an asset may be worth in the future.
- Economics addresses the production, distribution, and consumption of goods and services.
- Accounting communicates an organization's financial information and is really a backward-looking field.

These intertwining fields can be managed to bring value to organizations in volatile and uncertain markets.

Finance and accounting in turbulent times

Today's finance leaders accelerate transformation, bringing overall value to organizations through finance and accounting operations that address volatile and uncertain markets. These new financial leaders need agile finance organizations to support their enterprises, allowing them to cope efficiently and effectively with change.

Since 2007 and the onset of the greatest economic depression in two generations, the world has become much more complex and unpredictable. In the wake of 2011's disastrous earthquake and tsunami in Japan, many international businesses learned that global supply chains, markets and customers have never been more vulnerable to events on the other side of the world. Financial management is central to the successful navigation of global businesses through these uncertain times as the function that allocates funding for growth and controls expense management.

What is required today is a new generation of chief financial officers (CFOs) to transform the function to support strong, flexible and scalable global operating models, allowing organizations to grasp advantage and growth when surrounded by volatility and uncertainty.

However, that requires a fundamental shift in perspective, a commitment to global growth and a renewed focus on cost controls, the intelligent integration of acquisitions, and professional financial management that can adapt flexibly to fast-changing market conditions.

The influence of IT

The fundamental business disciplines of finance, economics and accounting have evolved since people first began to trade with neighbours – and those further afield – and to take account of the difference between what was bought, hunted, farmed or made, and then subsequently sold – profit! Although counting began with basic support, such as the abacus, it soon evolved into faster counting systems using logarithms, slide rules, calculators and, most latterly, computing. The information technology (IT) discipline started in accounts departments but soon began to permeate every other business discipline.

Today IT is a discrete business department, separate yet helping to underpin the management of all departments and communications, and intimately connected still with counting and understanding the flows of finance that lubricate all businesses.

'Bean-counters'

The scathing term 'bean-counters' is still often used derogatively and broadly to describe all financial, accounting and economic functions, probably to caricature a rather fussy and pedantic accountant responsible for knowing not just the weight of a bag of beans but exactly how many beans were in the bag! The US newspaper *The Fort Wayne News and Sentinel* is often attributed with the first use of the term, in an article in 1919.

Today's finance, economics and accounting functions in businesses are transforming their organizations' abilities to support strong, flexible and scalable global operating models, allowing them to grasp advantage and growth when surrounded by environments that are volatile and uncertain. And yet the very technology – information technology – that has enormously helped financial controls to demonstrate and supervise these flows of money in organizations is often described as one of the principal causes of volatility in economics and finance today. In fact, however, IT controls are used now by stock markets to reduce damaging surges in volatile world markets.

The changing role of the CFO

Ernst and Young (now EY) conducted research and developed a report with very interesting insights into the views of the world by today's chief financial officers (CFOs).

You can access this report at www.ey.com/GL/en/Issues/
Managing-finance/The-DNA-of-the-CFO---perspectives-on-
the-evolving-role. The report suggests that the role of CFOs
is developing rapidly, in terms of:

- the scope of their responsibilities
- the skillsets required for the role
- the development of future CFOs
- the career aspirations of today's CFOs.

> *'As CFO, I'm in a unique position within the
> organization, at the absolute center of the
> universe. The only other executive besides me
> that has that same presence at
> the center is the CEO.'*
>
> Bruce Besanko, OfficeMax, quoted in 'The DNA of the CFO'

Alongside their traditional role of providing financial insight
and analysis, CFOs are becoming increasingly involved in
supporting and even developing strategy, guiding key business
initiatives. For this reason, the report says, CFOs 'must be
versatile individuals with the talent to meet a continually
changing set of circumstances'. The CFO remains 'an objective
voice on financial performance but contributes to operational
decision-making as well. CFOs manage or materially support
information technology, investor relations, real estate and
strategic M&A — and some are involved in commercial activities.'

Some key findings of the EY report

- 'Most CFOs believe they have viable internal
  candidates to succeed them in their role, but few
  organizations have identified a specific candidate
  or have a formal plan to prepare their next CFO.'
- 'Communications skills are an imperative, as CFOs
  must convey complex financial results and
  business performance to external stakeholders
  while championing specific initiatives internally.'

From the report, it emerges that CFOs' primary concern is with two related issues:

1 having a complete view of the hierarchies of the most important financial data concerning their business
2 their abilities to derive the most insightful strategic kernels of important information from that data and to communicate that information effectively.

In this world of data, finding the 'truth' and communicating it effectively is what keeps CFOs awake at night.

An interesting relationship in many organizations – also revealed by the EY report – is that between the CFO and the top marketing executive. The statement that '[t]oday's CFOs must still attend closely to cash flows, controls, costs and risk [and at] the same time ... continue to seek profitable growth — both in mature markets and in those that hold the promise of rapid growth' indicates quite well where one set of business responsibilities ends and the other begins. The overlap is in finding growth.

Once the areas of potential growth have been found, usually through market research in its various forms, and the marketing function has determined how to reach and satisfy them (see Wednesday), then the CFO and his/her teams can work to bring them under good financial control. They will then create (along with the marketing department and the function that develops new products or services) forecasts for sales revenues, costs and profits, and thus justifications for investments or divestments, for the future profitable growth of their organizations.

Overlapping responsibilities

All business disciplines make claims about their leadership roles across many other disciplines, and CFOs' responsibilities can be argued to extend to the business areas usually covered by Human Resources (HR), Marketing and even the Legal Department:

'The CFO's role has always been a demanding one, but rapid developments in

regulation, information technology and the economy are defining a new era for the CFO, characterized by a significant expansion in his role and responsibilities. In these circumstances the success of the CFO and his ability to deliver on a broad agenda is contingent on the finance function's ability to establish strong relationships across the enterprise as well as with external stakeholders.'

Karen dela Torre, Vice President, Oracle Corporation

Dela Torre goes on to argue how the growth of statutory and regulatory reporting has stretched the finance function to the limit, as it seeks to absorb the changes without adding to headcount. As transaction volumes have expanded and business has become ever more complex, the finance function has become almost totally reliant on technology so that the relationship with IT is now crucial to success.

Chief information officers (CIOs), she points out, now commonly report directly to the CFO. It is worth recalling that, historically, the financial departments in companies often provided the genesis for the development of IT departments – Karen dela Torre describes this as coming full circle with IT once again falling under the responsibilities of the Finance Department!

It is interesting to examine these areas of overlapping responsibilities in the context of the changing of traditional roles in businesses. The Chartered Quality Institute in the UK has a relevant view:

'Organizations are made up of individuals brought together to enable the organization to achieve its mission. The organization's structure will determine how these individuals are brought together and how they relate to one another. The success of the

organization is dependent on each individual working together to achieve the common goal. If individuals are pulling in different directions, this will have a detrimental impact upon the organization achieving its mission. It is the role of the manager to integrate the activities of individuals, ensuring that they are aware of the institution's priorities and that they are working towards them. Managers achieve this through the authority delegated to them within the organization's hierarchy.'

The Chartered Quality Institute – www.thecqi.org

In other words, the Chief Executive and his or her board, in any organization, will define the extent, borders and overlaps of managers' responsibilities. If they decide that the Finance Department should have a degree of authority and control over areas normally managed by the HR function or by Marketing, for example, so long as these responsibilities are decided, clearly recorded and understood by all, there need be no misunderstanding or confusions about 'who does what'!

Pressures on financial functions

In the future development of the financial functions in organizations, there are several pressures that will force change. These include, as examples:

- The internationalization – globalization – of business, which brings with it different currencies and currency movements and differing legal requirements
- Changes in banking regulations, forced by the global downturn that started in 2007
- The geopolitical ambitions of leaders of countries such as China, Russia and North Korea, frequently causing problems

to international trade due to the placement of embargoes and trade restrictions

● Changes in information technology, which often create great efficiencies in financial operations but can create vulnerabilities to other, sometimes malign, organizations and countries

● Changes in the education of future CFOs, mostly owing to MOOCS – Massive Online Open Courses – in which most of the learning is done remotely, at PCs in students' rooms, without challenging face-to-face discussion.

Thus, changes to the structures and operating processes of financial departments are on their way, to accommodate some of the issues described above – and so are changes to the roles of CFOs.

Tools of the trade

Besides a general introduction to why and how financial departments work and are managed, and the future direction of the finance functions, an MBA degree also helps students to become familiar with the tools of the trade, the financial models and structures used commonly to calculate, display and communicate the financial situation of their companies, at any one time, to managers and others. These include:

● the balance sheet
● the profit and loss (P&L) account

- cash flow calculations
- researching accounts using ratio analysis.

Business plans – especially for small companies and start-ups – are often justifications for new strategies and financial investments. As such, a balance sheet, P&L and cash flow projections for the period under critical review are all vital components of the business plan.

> *'Owner managers today need to be able to understand finance; leaving everything to an accountant is easy, but isn't practical. The basics of finance are worth a bit of effort to learn and understand, as you can glean invaluable business information. [...] Effective control requires effective planning and target setting but it also requires an understanding of financial statements and an ability to interpret the figures.'*
>
> Shell LiveWIRE – shell-livewire.org

Ratio analysis

Ratio analysis (RA) is a cornerstone of fundamental, financial and corporate analysis. It is a quantitative analysis of information from a company's financial statements, the line items in the balance sheet, profit and loss account and cash flow statements. The ratios of an item to another item, or combination of items, are calculated and used to evaluate the company's operating and financial performance, for example its efficiency, liquidity, profitability and solvency. Trends in these ratios, studied over time, give important insights into the changing situation and, when compared to those of other companies in the same sector, provide views on comparative performances and valuations.

Understanding how the CFO and the world of financial controls works, the balance sheet, the profit and loss account, cash-flow projections, ratio analysis and their place in business planning, are all critical studies for the business manager and well worth a few hours of extra MBA studies!

MBA recommended reading list

Jason Karaian, *The Chief Financial Officer: What CFOs Do, the Influence They Have and Why It Matters* (Economist Books, 2014)

Roger Mason, *Bookkeeping and Accounting In A Week* (John Murray Learning, 2016)

Hunter Muller, *The Big Shift in IT Leadership: How Great CIOs Leverage the Power of Technology for Strategic Business Growth* (Wiley, 2015)

Summary

Descriptions of drivers of change often emphasize new technology and that is certainly a major force. However, in order to embed the new technology and to harness it to accelerate an organization's progress, managers need wide-ranging skill sets and that is why MBA degrees are taught in business schools to experienced executives midway through their careers. CFOs need to understand and be able to view the organization holistically – to see it in the round – and to not only view their business world through spread sheets, balance sheets, and profit and loss accounts.

SUNDAY
MONDAY
TUESDAY
WEDNESDAY
THURSDAY
FRIDAY
SATURDAY

Fact-check (answers at the back)

1. How do finance, economics and accounting support world markets?
   a) By bringing stability to volatile markets ❏
   b) By reducing insolvencies ❏
   c) From fostering an understanding cash flows in international companies ❏
   d) By keeping a tight control of costs in organizations ❏

2. What may cause the greatest risks to world stock markets?
   a) A global company becoming bankrupt ❏
   b) Sudden and catastrophic events causing disruption to global supply chains ❏
   c) Changes in international interest rates ❏
   d) New governments taking control in countries with large world economies ❏

3. What will be the greatest challenge to future CFOs?
   a) To control costs in times of great variations in interest rates ❏
   b) To avoid corruption and the infiltration of fraud and criminal activities ❏
   c) To control salaries and reward structures to maintain motivation but minimize costs ❏
   d) To transform financial functions to support strong, flexible and scalable global operating models in conditions of volatility and uncertainty ❏

4. How might you best describe the present-day accounting function in an organization?
   a) Today's CFOs have a much more central role in broad corporate decision-making ❏
   b) Accounting functions should be kept separate from other parts of the enterprise to preserve their independence and authority ❏
   c) CFOs have an important role in enterprises but one that is subservient to the other disciplines such as marketing or operations ❏
   d) Accounting functions are becoming subservient to HR departments as a way of controlling salaries ❏

5. What are the critical financial statements expected in any business plan?
   a) Budget statements for future capital expenditures ❏
   b) A balance sheet, P&L and cash flow projection for the period under critical review ❏
   c) A view of discounted cash flow statements on key capital investments ❏
   d) A summary of the business's strategy and its likely trajectory ❏

6. How did the IT departments in most businesses begin to take shape?
a) When Microsoft first created Windows software suites ❑
b) Only after IBM initiated business software and sold accounting packages to companies' accounts departments ❑
c) They arose out of accounts departments and thence began to permeate every other business discipline ❑
d) From a need to count profits more accurately ❑

7. What is a root cause of volatility in financial markets?
a) Globalized companies having to trade in many different currencies ❑
b) The integration and maintenance of old legacy IT systems controlling financial operations ❑
c) IT systems and controls used by stock markets to reduce damaging surges ❑
d) Fraud and criminal activities ❑

8. Which of the following are examples of pressures forcing change in the future development of the financial functions in organizations?
a) Changes in banking regulations, forced by the global downturn that started in 2007 ❑
b) New financial governance requirements in the United States ❑
c) The growing international use of Bitcoins ❑
d) Reduction of global interest rates ❑

9. Why is there a now a requirement for new critical relationships across organizations, usually involving CFOs?
a) The CFO's role and responsibilities are expanding ❑
b) There are new international legal requirements ❑
c) There are new international auditing standards ❑
d) The education of future CFOs is being negatively affected by the growth of MOOCs ❑

10. Developments in information technology are leading to changes in the financial functions in organizations. How might this be reflected?
a) In higher IT budgets ❑
b) In opportunities for new revenue streams and novel ways of engaging with customers ❑
c) In the increasing organizational separation of IT departments and financial operations ❑
d) In more subcontracting of the IT function (e.g. 'cloud' computing) ❑

SUNDAY

MONDAY

TUESDAY

WEDNESDAY

THURSDAY

FRIDAY

SATURDAY

TUESDAY

Entrepreneurship, ethics and social responsibility

Many MBA students ask for the definitions of, and differences between, ethics and morals. Ethics and morals both make judgements on human behaviours that are either 'right' or 'wrong'. However, ethics is a set of rules given to an individual by another body or organization such as their business (known as 'business ethics'), profession or religion. Morals refer to an individual's own principles regarding right and wrong – their 'moral compass'. Business ethics and social responsibility are very important in entrepreneurial ventures, particularly in decision-making processes.

An ethical mind-frame assists entrepreneurs in making the best decisions for the longer term in fast-moving and complex entrepreneurial environments. A strong sense of social responsibility helps entrepreneurs to make decisions that best enhance benefits and decrease risks for stakeholders and investors in entrepreneurial organizations.

Why be ethical in business?

Business ethics examines ethical principles in business environments and all aspects of business conduct, and relates to how the individuals in businesses and entire business organizations behave with respect to one other and to their external worlds.

Business ethics consists of written and unwritten codes of values, principles and practices that guide the corporate culture – the principles upon which decisions and actions are made in a business. In the business world, business ethics are an agreed, common understanding in companies of the difference between right and wrong practices.

Businesses should be run according to their business and strategic plans, which should always be living documents, a part of daily business life and the touchstone and foundation for all complex decision making. A business's policies should be bounded by their ethical principles and frameworks.

Social responsibility, as a subject in today's business world, means doing what is morally right and behaving 'unto others as you would have them behave unto you'. This 'Golden Rule' is integral to ethical principles and behaviours. The International

Standards Organization (ISO) gives the following definition of 'social responsibility':

'The responsibility of an organization for the impacts of its decisions and activities on society and the environment, through transparent and ethical behaviour that:

- *contributes to sustainable development, including health and the welfare of society*
- *takes into account the expectations of stakeholders*
- *is in compliance with applicable laws and consistent with international norms of behaviour*
- *is integrated throughout the organization and practised in its relationships.'*

ISO 26000: *Guidance on Social Responsibility*, 2010.

Neglect of business ethics and groupthink

There have been occasions, historically, when some entrepreneurial and dynamic businesses thought that sacrificing ethics and social responsibilities would offer a short cut to increased profitable growth. Such an attitude is fast disappearing. According to the US-based audio-visual and event technology services company Meeting Tomorrow (http://www.meetingtomorrow.com/cms-category/business-ethics-and-social-responsibility), drawing on research from the American Management Association, '56 per cent of surveyed participants ranked ethical behaviour as the most important characteristics of effective leaders'. It goes on to point out:

'Americans have witnessed first-hand the destruction that occurs when corporations do not behave ethically. Businesses who conduct themselves in an ethical manner pass their values, morals, and beliefs down to the employees and customers. The effect can be felt throughout the community, which has a profound impact on local schools, community centers, and other groups. Companies such as Enron, Tyco, Adelphia, and WorldCom are classic examples of what can happen when corporations disregard or neglect the importance of business ethics. A company's ethical behaviour can build or destroy Main Street USA.'

The Enron Scandal

The case of Enron in 2001 is the perfect illustration of the effects described above. At the beginning of the new millennium Enron was one of the United States' best-known and most successful companies, employing some 20,000 staff and with revenues of almost $111 billion. At the end of 2001, however, Enron's 'success' was shown to be an illusion, created by a sustained and systematic campaign of corporate fraud and corruption. The resulting scandal threw into question the accounting practices of many US corporations and helped lead to the passing of the Sarbanes–Oxley Act of 2002, which set out stringent new standards and responsibilities for public companies in the United States.

The Enron Scandal is an example of a large and entrepreneurial organization neglecting ethics and social responsibility and coming completely unstuck because of that management failure.

Another illustrative example is that of WorldCom, a US company found guilty, in 2002, of accounting irregularities of $11 billion and which subsequently filed for bankruptcy. Analysis of WorldCom's demise suggests that its endemic unethical behaviours were the result of **groupthink**, defined by the US psychologist Irving Janis as a

'mode of thinking that people engage in when they are deeply involved in a cohesive in-group, when the members' strivings for unanimity override their motivation to realistically appraise alternative courses of action.'

Janis pointed to notable examples of groupthink outside the business sphere – President Kennedy's decision to invade Cuba at the Bay of Pigs and the US decision to escalate to war in Vietnam – but also showed how corporate groupthink can have deeply destructive effects within business, too. Feelings of invulnerability, refusal to accept dissent, and self-censorship within the group lead to extremely poor decision making.

The description above of how 'groupthink' within company culture can skew both individuals' moral compasses and whole organizations' business ethics indicates not only how serious but also insidious this corporate error of management judgement can become.

Whistleblowers

But how should company laws concerning ethics be policed? This can, in part, be addressed by 'whistleblowers'.

'Whistleblowing is when a worker reports suspected wrongdoing at work. Officially, this is called "making a disclosure in the public interest".

A worker can report things that aren't right, are illegal or if anyone at work is neglecting their duties, including:

- *someone's health and safety is in danger*
- *damage to the environment*
- *a criminal offence*
- *the company isn't obeying the law (e.g. not having the right insurance)*
- *covering up wrongdoing.'*

www.gov.uk/whistleblowing

It is important for a business to develop a coherent, objective approach to the issue of whistleblowing, since the actions of a whistleblower can cause disruption in the workplace, inflict serious harm on individuals wrongly accused, and have important financial consequences for a business. A UK survey showed that a little more than half of whistleblowing incidents resulted in external investigations of the companies involved, and more than one-fifth in criminal investigations.

Failure to respond to whistleblowers' concerns, or indeed showing outright hostility, should never have been acceptable, but in today's world are likely to be even more destructive. Merely kicking an incident into the long grass by, for example, dismissing the whistleblower is not an option. Companies who adopt this strategy are increasingly facing legal proceedings – and ultimately large financial penalties as well as poor publicity – as the former employee sues for wrongful dismissal.

The UK government whistleblowing website cited above suggests three ways in which companies can handle whistleblowing effectively and constructively:

1 Employees 'must be informed of the appropriate steps to take in communicating their ethical concerns internally'.
2 Employees 'must believe that their concerns will be taken seriously and will be investigated'.

3 Employees 'must feel confident that they will not suffer personal reprisals for using internal channels to report perceived wrongdoing'.

In this way, companies can provide internal mechanisms that promote critical self-reflection and ethical business development.

Non-executive directors (NEDs)

There is another and parallel means that can be deployed to keep organizations' business cultures on track: the use of non-executive directors (NEDs) on companies' management boards of directors, as a kind of 'internal whistleblowing'. Evidence suggests, however, that the effectiveness of NEDs in this respect can be a mixed bag. While NEDs will certainly have challenged executive decisions and from time to time successfully exposed serious problems, there are also likely to be instances where they have avoided taking action for fear of personal consequences. Moreover, the value of their work where they do challenge corporate behaviours is diminished because it does not become public knowledge and cannot therefore inform public debate.

Thus, while NEDs provide a valuable service in companies today, their positions must be strongly supported by chief executives in order that they can maintain their principled, balanced and independent view of the organizations' practices. This service can then provide a valuable supporting bulwark to maintain organizations' practices concerning business ethics and social responsibility.

Corporate governance

Since the corporate scandals of the beginning of the Millennium (see above) and the financial crisis that began in 2007–8 there has been an upsurge in interest in the corporate governance practices of modern corporations, especially in relation to **accountability**.

The term 'corporate governance' refers to the business activities and processes designed to control and direct the behaviours of corporations to align and balance the interests of their stakeholders. These stakeholders include shareholders, management, customers, suppliers, financiers, government and the broader community served, and focuses on the rules and procedures for making decisions in corporate affairs. Managers of organizations may be tempted to make decisions that benefit themselves but may harm others. Corporate governance examines the processes that set corporations' objectives and implement them in social, regulatory and market environments and include observation of the activities, policies and decision making in corporations.

THE BUCK STOPS HERE

Thus, good corporate governance embeds in organizations mechanisms that monitor and regulate the organizations' adherence to their own guidelines on corporate culture, business ethics and social responsibility:

'Effective corporate governance requires balanced boards made up of people with the right skills operating in a transparent and accountable framework. Good practice

should be shared across businesses but laying down inflexible rules can result in a tick-box approach, forcing businesses to adopt frameworks that don't work for them and does nothing to improve outcomes.'

Confederation of British Industry (CBI) – http://news.cbi.org.uk

Case study: Coca-Cola

We will conclude today with a discussion of a company with a highly developed and transparent approach to corporate responsibility and business ethics: Coca-Cola.

'We [Coca-Cola] are guided by our established standards of corporate governance and ethics. We review our systems to ensure we achieve international best practices in terms of transparency and accountability. The foundation of our approach to corporate governance is laid out in our Corporate Governance Guidelines and in the charters of our Board of Directors' committees.'

www.coca-colacompany.com/our-company/
governance-ethics/governance-ethics

Key aspects of Coca-Cola's multi-pronged approach include:

- The management of corporate responsibility through its **Public Policy and Corporate Reputation Council,** a cross-functional group of senior managers from the company and its partners: 'The Council identifies risks and opportunities faced by our business and communities and recommends strategies to address these challenges.'
- A **Code of Business Conduct** that demands of directors, associates and employees 'honesty and integrity in all matters'.

- The overseeing of the Code by an **Ethics and Compliance Committee**, another cross-functional senior management team.
- An **Ethics and Compliance Office** that has 'operational responsibility for education, consultation, monitoring and assessment related to the Code of Business Conduct and compliance issues'.
- **Training courses** for associates and employees worldwide to ensure an ongoing commitment to and understanding of the Code of Business Conduct. In 2010 some 22,000 employees were certified as being in compliance with the Code and Coca-Cola's anti-bribery requirements. On average, employees receive an average of 60 minutes' ethics training every year.

Coca-Cola's complex, global approach shows how seriously organizations today take the subjects of business ethics and corporate and social responsibility. Tackling this issue head on is not for the faint-hearted but the lessons of not doing so, from Enron, WorldCom and others, are still comparatively recent and fresh in the memory.

MBA recommended reading list

Mick Blowfield and Alan Murray, *Corporate Responsibility*, 4th edition (Oxford University Press, 2014)

Andrew Crane and Dirk Matten, *Business Ethics: Managing Corporate Citizenship and Sustainability in the Age of Globalization*, 3rd edition (Oxford University Press, 2010)

Peter Elkind and Bethany MacLean, *The Smartest Guys in the Room: The Amazing Rise and Scandalous Fall of Enron* (Penguin, 2004)

Summary

Business ethics and social responsibility are very important in entrepreneurial ventures and a strong sense of social responsibility helps entrepreneurs to make decisions that best enhance benefits and decrease risks for stakeholders and investors in entrepreneurial organizations. A case study of a company that chose the wrong operational paths – Enron – was examined as was an example of a company with an exemplary ethical framework – Coca-Cola.

'Whistleblowing' by employees in organizations and the probable benefit of having non-executive directors on company boards were also discussed. Today activist shareholders and investors also make headlines when they try to change corporate behaviours in companies they target.

These activities are all focused on trying to create and maintain patterns and systems of corporate behaviour and the ways in which organizations are run for the better – in the views of stakeholders, employees, the laws under which they should operate and society at large.

SUNDAY
MONDAY
TUESDAY
WEDNESDAY
THURSDAY
FRIDAY
SATURDAY

Fact-check (answers at the back)

1. Which of the following best describes business ethics?
   a) Rules for business set by governments ❑
   b) Guidelines for responsible managers given by a relevant business body or authority ❑
   c) Business guidelines set by trade associations ❑
   d) Common sense and a knowledge of the law ❑

2. How might you define 'morality' in business?
   a) Legally binding business laws ❑
   b) Operational guidelines for businesses in each business sector ❑
   c) A manager's own business principles regarding the right and the wrong ways in which to operate his or her business – their 'moral compass' ❑
   d) Obeying the law and treating people as you would expect to be treated ❑

3. What does the term 'social responsibility' mean in today's business world?
   a) Being honest and truthful in the use of social media ❑
   b) Looking after the best interests of employees in a business ❑
   c) A subject integral to ethical principles and behaviours in business life ❑
   d) Being as good as your word and keeping your promises to employees ❑

4. How would you best describe the example provided by Enron?
   a) A well-known example of wilful corporate fraud and corruption ❑
   b) A scandal brought about by insider trading ❑
   c) The result of the creation of the Sarbanes–Oxley Act ❑
   d) This is how business has always behaved until caught out ❑

5. What is groupthink?
   a) A kind of mutiny among the directors of a company against the CEO ❑
   b) A strategy to determine a new corporate direction ❑
   c) A group of managers skewing their moral compasses together by a subconscious common agreement ❑
   d) When groups of people who work closely together take decisions in concert ❑

6. What activity, from the early outset in the formation of any company, is vital for the safe future conduct of that company?
   a) Agreement of the CEO's package of rewards ❑
   b) The setting down of written and unwritten codes of values, principles and practices that guide corporate culture ❑
   c) The recruitment of a Chief Ethics Officer ❑
   d) Writing the corporate business plan ❑

7. What is 'whistleblowing'?
a) Where a worker reports suspected wrongdoing at work ❑
b) Where trades union leaders call a strike in the workplace ❑
c) A reliable backup when the fire alarm system fails ❑
d) Telling tales and betraying loyalties ❑

8. Why do companies use non-executive directors (NEDs) on their management board of directors?
a) To check that remuneration of the board of directors is fair ❑
b) Because they are cheaper to employ than executive directors ❑
c) Because NEDs are often able to effectively challenge executive decisions to keep organizations' business cultures on track ❑
d) NEDs are used only on the boards of charities ❑

9. In some situations, NEDs have not been able to challenge executive decisions or expose serious problems. Why might this be so?
a) Because they do not have the authority ❑
b) Because they are not invited to key board meetings ❑
c) Because sometimes they may be fearful of the personal consequences they may suffer ❑
d) Because they fear that the potential repercussions do not balance at their pay-grade ❑

10. What is the Code of Business Conduct at the Coca-Cola Company?
a) A committee that sets the agreed formulae for Coca-Cola's drinks in international bottling plants ❑
b) A way to ensure that workers' conditions are managed equably around the world ❑
c) A guide for all the company's associates and directors requiring honesty and integrity in all matters ❑
d) A way of ensuring that product is not pilfered and drunk on the premises ❑

SUNDAY

MONDAY

TUESDAY

WEDNESDAY

THURSDAY

FRIDAY

SATURDAY

WEDNESDAY

Strategy and marketing

Strategic planning is concerned with the overall direction of the business. It is allied with marketing and makes decisions about production and operations, finance, human resources and all business issues. Marketing management is key in strategic planning because it must understand and manage the connections between the business and the marketplace. At the heart of strategic planning are the questions:

- Where are we now?
- How did we get there?
- Where are we heading?
- Where would we like to be?
- How do we get there?
- What barriers lie ahead?
- How do we overcome them?
- Are we on course?

A natural marriage

Strategic management and marketing are completely intertwined. Yet, for many managers who are untrained in marketing, marketing is a discipline that is synonymous with advertising and promotion. Because of this perception, many businesspeople believe that marketing is an unlikely bedfellow with a 'heavyweight' subject such as the determination of business strategy.

However, marketing is a much broader and more all-encompassing discipline than promotion, which is simply just a very visible component part of the subject of marketing. Marketing and strategy run together because marketing must understand and manage the connections between their business and the marketplace and strategy must relate the business and its operations to the marketplace and customers. Thus, strategic management and marketing are a natural pairing of business activities with an interlocking fit.

Building and using business models and frameworks is a subject addressed later in this chapter and is an area of business activity that is fundamental to obtaining and maintaining strategic direction.

The close relationship between strategic management and marketing can be seen in the way that strategic decisions are responses to strategic questions about how the organization will compete. For example:

- Who is the target customer for the organization's products and services?
- Where are the customers located and how do they buy the organization's products and services?
- In the eyes of customers and other stakeholders, what makes the organization stand out from its competitors?
- What are the key opportunities and risks for the organization?
- How can the organization grow, both in terms of its base business and new business?
- How can the organization generate more value for investors?

These questions and others like them suggest how a deep understanding of the external environment and a business's markets is critical to the strategic planning process.

Strategies for growth

The determination of business strategy as a subject first appeared in the 1950s and 1960s, in the work of academics such as Peter Drucker, H. Igor Ansoff, Bruce Henderson, Philip Selznick and Alfred Chandler. A major preoccupation of the period was in the determination of organizations' SWOTs (Strengths – Weaknesses – Opportunities – Threats).

SWOT analysis

The origins of SWOT analysis are unclear but this planning method, used to determine an organization's (or project's) strengths, weaknesses, opportunities and threats, had become established by the 1960s.

First the objective of the organization or project is identified and then the factors that are favourable and unfavourable for the achievement of that objective, both internal (the characteristics of the organization) and external (the characteristics of the environment) analysed:

Strengths: characteristics of the organization or project that give it an advantage over others	**Weaknesses:** characteristics that place the business or project at a disadvantage relative to others
Opportunities: elements that the project could exploit to its advantage	**Threats:** elements in the environment that could cause trouble for the business or project

The term 'strategic fit' is used to describe the match between the characteristics of the organization and the environment.

In the 1960s there was a heated debate over the risks that companies should take in pursuit of new opportunities (diversification), at the risk of sacrificing their existing competencies. In a classic 1960 article, 'Marketing Myopia', the US economist Theodore Levitt (1935–2006), for example, criticized businesses firms that were too inward-looking, focused on delivering an established product rather than seeking to meet customer's changing needs. When companies fail, he wrote,

> *'it usually means that the product fails to adapt to the constantly changing patterns of consumer needs and tastes, to new and modified marketing institutions and practices, or to product developments in complementary industries.'*

Theodore Levitt, 'Marketing Myopia', *Harvard Business Review* (1960)

The Russian-born applied mathematician Igor Ansoff (1918–2002) – the 'father of strategic management' – argued that more caution was required when companies diversified; Levitt, Ansoff thought, was simply asking companies to take too much risk by investing in new products that might not fit the firm's distinctive competence. Instead, he believed, a company needs to identify whether any new product grows naturally out of its existing ones – that there is a 'common thread' between them. Just because its customers have needs other than those already being met by the company does not mean that it is necessarily in a position to diversify to meet them.

To help companies to identify the relative risks they face as they seek to grow, Ansoff developed the Product/Market Growth Matrix, well known to all MBA students!

The Ansoff Growth Matrix

The Ansoff Growth Matrix is an essential tool in strategic planning to find opportunities for growth:

- by increased penetration of existing markets with current products or services
- by new product or service development
- by entering new markets with current products or services, *or*
- by complete diversification into the relative unknown by entering new markets with new products or services.

	Existing products	New products
Existing markets	Market penetration	Product development
New markets	Market development	Diversification

These strategies for growth are all related to risk. However, the greatest risk (and source of potential opportunity!) lies in diversification – introducing new products or services to new markets.

Besides growth strategies, others also exist, although most businesses focus on strategies to deliver profitable growth, rather than to accept the status quo or decline!

The descriptions of the development of strategic thinking above demonstrate very clearly the intimate, close relationship between the disciplines of strategic development and marketing. It has become accepted that any business strategy that looks only inwards at its own distinctive competencies without taking into account the positions and attitudes of its actual and potential customers can ultimately lead only to failure.

Business modelling

'A business model is the means to define why the organization exists and how it creates, delivers, and captures value.'
Dan Olszewski

An awareness of how business models have evolved over the last five decades or so is vital for any MBA student. Business models are the frameworks of how businesses operate to make sales revenues and profits. Business models are designed when a business is launched but they usually also evolve and improve over time. In *The Business Model Canvas* (2010), Yves Pigneur and Alexander Osterwalder describe how to build and how to improve business models for startups through to mature organizations.

Examples of business models developed by businesses in recent decades are:

The 1960s

- **Oldsmobile** (General Motors) relied upon new product development (e.g. turbocharged engines) and the frequent introduction of new vehicle designs.
- In 1959 **American Airlines** teamed up with IBM to introduce the SABRE (Semi-Automated Business Research Environment), a huge electronic data-processing system that created and managed airline seat reservations and instantly made that data available.

The 1970s

- Fred Smith wrote a paper for an economics class as an undergraduate at Yale University which proposed an overnight delivery service in which one carrier is responsible for a piece of cargo from pick-up through delivery by flying all of its own aircraft, operating its own depots, posting stations and delivery vans. At this time cargo shipment was handled by a chain of companies and Smith's idea was unorthodox – he got a C grade for his paper. Smith, however, went on to found **Federal Express** in the early 1970s. After early financial difficulties and improvements to the business model, Smith's personal wealth today is about $2 billion!

- **Toys Я Us** developed its profile as the 'world's greatest toy store', bar none. The stores were packed with every toy and kids' entertainment product imaginable. Walking up and down the long warehouse-style aisles to view items from bicycles to dolls to crafts and building sets was an entertainment in itself. This was a complete retail business model for the child.

The 1980s

- The first **Blockbuster** store opened in1985 in Texas, founded by David Cook from his background in managing huge databases. Early success was built on customizing a store to its local population's demographics, with films geared specifically to their profiles, popular new releases and lots of catalogue titles. Blockbuster's business model fell victim to Netflix and Redbox in 2010.

- **Home Depot** set up huge stores, with the best possible customer service, helping customers to lay tiles, change valves or use power tools. All customer-facing staff underwent rigorous product training and the stores held clinics to teach customers how to do it themselves. This revolutionized the DIY industry, teaching know-how and bringing the customers the tools to do the job and saving them money.

- In the early 1980s **Intel**'s business was in DRAM memory chips. Strong Japanese competition significantly reduced the DRAM market's profitability by 1983 and the success of the IBM PC motivated CEO Andy Grove to focus on microprocessors and to fundamentally change the company business model. This change of strategy was successful and Intel was set on a ten-year course of profitable growth as the leading hardware supplier to the PC industry in the 1980s and 1990s. Fierce competition in the semiconductor industry has since diminished its position.

- Michael Dell upgraded his IBM-compatible PC in his room in 1983 at the University of Texas. He quickly realized that he could buy components and assemble PCs more cheaply himself instead of upgrading older machines. He began to sell the PCS with the **Dell** name on it directly to customers at a 15-per-cent discount to established brands. He started advertising in trade magazines and grew the order book. Within a year, he dropped out of college to run his business full time and in 1984 his business officially became Dell Computer Corporation.

The 1990s

- **Southwest Airlines** primary focus has remained short point-to-point flights. By only flying one type of aircraft, it is has a heavier flight schedule than its competitors because loading and unloading of its aircrafts is completely standardized. Staff and pilots have to learn only one set of skills used repeatedly. Only one type of specialized equipment is required to service and maintain the airplane fleet. Many airlines have attempted to emulate Southwest but it has developed a niche. This business model has allowed Southwest to succeed in the airline industry and it will be difficult for rival airlines to adopt this business model individually to increase productivity.

- The founders of **Netflix** realized that they could send CDs through the US Postal Service without damaging them. The DVD rental-by-mail business put Netflix on the map. In 1997 the video rental market was dominated by Blockbuster and others renting VHS titles. Netflix made a series of smart and lucky decisions to dominate the video rental industry. They first partnered with manufacturers of DVD players to develop consumer interest in this new format, increasing its adoption and gaining visibility for their brand. Then Netflix contacted the film studios to position their service as a market-enhancing proposition. With luck and good fortune, Netflix entered the market just as it became ready for them, and their risks were limited.

- The 'growth first, revenue later' is a risky business model, but a proven one. The high level of risk is one reason why the returns can be so great. Although it is commonly held that **Amazon**'s business model operates in this way, in fact the company does not fit this mould. Founded in 1995 and holding its initial public offering (IPO) in 1997, it is certainly not a firm without revenue or a clear revenue strategy. At the website you can find items you want to buy and they have prices next to them. If you want to buy, you enter your credit card information and buy them. It's the most boring revenue strategy in the world and one of the oldest. It works! This firm remains a darling of Wall Street despite a lack of profitability. But Amazon doesn't turn a profit because it's a darling of Wall Street. Amazon is essentially the beneficiary of large Wall Street trends in its ability to eschew profits, yet it's also bucking the trend among its peer technology giants.
- The real business model for **Starbucks** was real estate. Selling coffee was simply the means to acquire prime commercial real estate. It was the real estate, and not the coffee, that increased shareholder value and made them wealthy. In the 1990s stock analysts understood that Starbucks' model caused the company to increase in value only by opening new stores, although that was never the source of Starbucks' growth. Coffee revenue was simply fed back into Starbucks' real-estate acquisitions, and this is what caused its stock value to explode. Recently, Starbucks began to lose its magic because the world has become overrun with Starbucks. As this business model succeeds, it inherently hits a point of diminishing returns.

The 2000s

- 'One Ford – One Team – One Plan – One Goal.' **Ford**'s 'One Ford' business plan was announced by Ford management in June 2008 as gas prices surged to the highest levels seen on record. The Ford plan, as outlined later that year to the US Senate, identified that the company needed to streamline its operation by unifying its global business. Ford stated that 'six European small vehicles [would be] coming to North America from global B-car and C-car platforms'. B-car models are subcompacts and C-car models are compacts.

- With the relatively recent passing of Steve Jobs, a lingering and much discussed question remains: what will happen to **Apple** without Jobs in charge? How will the company's business model change without Jobs to direct the company into new sectors? How long can Jobs's vision last? The company's business model is volatile. With Tim Cook at the top, new strategies may steer Apple away from Jobs's vision fairly quickly. Cook may do so by changing the company's supply chain, its marketing strategy, its market position, or its pricing strategy. We must watch and wait but the business model is changing...

MBA recommended reading list

Robert S. Kaplan and David P. Norton, *The Balanced Scorecard: Translating Strategy into Action* (Harvard Business Review Press, 1996)

Tom Osenton, *The Death of Demand: Finding Growth in a Saturated Global Economy* (Financial Times Prentice Hall Books, 2004)

Alexander Osterwalder and Yves Pigneur, *The Business Model Generator: A Handbook for Visionaries, Game Changers, and Challengers* (John Wiley & Sons, 2010)

Summary

Marketing management is key in strategic planning for businesses in order to understand, manage and make sense of the connections between their businesses and marketplaces. Strategic planning asks the key questions to position the business. To answer these questions, businesses conduct market research and that research includes intelligence on their competition, their political, social and economic environments and technologies. This information feeds directly into strategic planning, to illuminate the road ahead and all the barriers to their progress towards their objectives.

Testing out ideas for the strategic plan by using business models greatly reduces business risk. Business models prompt the questions to identify risk and to shine a light into any dark and forgotten corners of the business, illuminating issues that may have been previously overlooked, all before starting to trade. Today social media and the Internet offer tools for business managers to investigate with confidence the wants and needs of their actual or targeted customers to determine business models that work well, quickly and effectively.

SUNDAY
MONDAY
TUESDAY
WEDNESDAY
THURSDAY
FRIDAY
SATURDAY

Fact-check (answers at the back)

1. Why is marketing management key in strategic planning?
   a) Because marketing management brings the voice and needs of the customers and the marketplace into the overall management of the business ❏
   b) Because marketing management also manages the sales function ❏
   c) Because the design and strategies used in advertising and marketing communications must match corporate strategies ❏
   d) Because marketing management understands the competition ❏

2. SWOT analysis is still a very popular tool in strategic analysis. However, in what way does SWOT fail to guide us?
   a) It over-emphasizes weaknesses over strengths ❏
   b) It requires a great deal of very precise information to be useful ❏
   c) It does not bring closure to the problem of actually defining a firm's distinctive competence ❏
   d) It does not provide direct solutions to the issues raised ❏

3. In his article 'Marketing Myopia' (1960), Theodore Levitt argued what?
   a) That customers are notoriously fickle and firms should be wary of investing without thorough customer research ❏
   b) That firms seemed to focus too much on delivering a product ❏
   c) That supply chain efficiencies were critical for profitable growth ❏
   d) That all marketing is subject to myopic vision ❏

4. In new product development theory, H. Igor Ansoff argued that...
   a) New products should copy competitors' products as 'me toos' ('I have the same product also') to reduce risk ❏
   b) New product development should be left to R&D departments with little involvement from marketing departments being necessary ❏
   c) A company should first ask whether a new product had a 'common thread' with its existing products ❏
   d) That 'diversification' is too risky a strategy to be undertaken ❏

5. The purpose of business modelling is to...
a) Check that all the elements of the business are in place ❑
b) Define why the organization exists and how it creates, delivers and captures value ❑
c) Demonstrate the business's operations to investors ❑
d) Check the business against competitors' operations ❑

6. In the 1960s American Airlines' business model was...
a) Focused on aeronautical engineering and new aircraft designs ❑
b) A failure, requiring reinvestment ❑
c) Centred on the development of new engines and better fuel consumption ❑
d) Involved a new approach using IT technology to better plan seating reservations ❑

7. Federal Express was created in the 1970s but its business model was...
a) An instant success ❑
b) Judged a failure even by Fred Smith, the entrepreneur who started it up ❑
c) An eventual success, following improvements made to the original business model over time ❑
d) Completely overhauled ❑

8. In the 1990s Netflix's business model was...
a) The complete result of lucky decisions ❑
b) A failure, due to an intervention by Blockbuster ❑
c) Successful, due in part to a technological partnership ❑
d) A failure due to their relationship with the postal authority ❑

9. Also in the 1990s Amazon
a) Introduced a 'growth first, revenue later' business model that failed badly ❑
b) Is a website-based, sales revenue business model ❑
c) Is unpopular today with Wall Street due to its lack of profits ❑
d) Has no clear revenue strategy ❑

10. In the 2000s Apple's business model...
a) Remains unchanged, following the death of Steve Jobs, its founder ❑
b) Will be soon ditched as the company is due to be taken over by Google ❑
c) Is likely to change especially with with respect to its supply chain ❑
d) Will remain static, as Tim Cook, the new head of Apple, is intolerant of change ❑

SUNDAY

MONDAY

TUESDAY

WEDNESDAY

THURSDAY

FRIDAY

SATURDAY

THURSDAY

Operations management

The term 'operations' is often used for the corporate area in businesses responsible for the production of goods or services. This includes all activities to create and deliver products or services, from procuring suppliers and materials to logistics and supply chain management (SCM). The operations area usually has the greatest number of assets and employees.

Operations as an area is also the foundation for the company's long-term performance because it is usually responsible for product or service quality and is frequently viewed as a source of competitive advantage. Managed well, operations helps to ensure that the organization's strategy is realized.

Making a difference

Together with marketing, operations departments breathe life into corporate strategy, preventing it from remaining just a theoretical exercise by creating and delivering the added value of the business. In 2014 PriceWaterhouseCoopers' (PwC) 17th Annual CEO survey found that broadening operation options for customers is a factor that drives differences in performance and that 71 per cent of US CEOs are planning to remake their fulfilment and service supply chains. The survey found three sources of leverage:

1 broadening service operation options for customers
2 engaging service supply chain partners in innovating operational practices
3 focusing on end-to-end performance in quality and management.

PwC's survey found that a vigorous focus on these activities, in the traditional area of operations management, can drive differences in performance and create increased competitive advantage.

Sourcing a workforce

There is, however, a major problem that hinders the success of operations departments, especially in organizations in the United States and Europe – the recruitment and retention of capable people. Moreover, since, as has already been noted, operations departments usually have the greatest number of employees, this makes recruitment an especially significant issue for organizations, especially smaller ones.

We might even speak of a recruitment crisis in the West, as middle-technology jobs, requiring only a middling level of skill and training, are leaving the United States and Europe for China and other Asian countries:

'I think we should recognize that the period between 1950 and 1980 was an unusual period in Western history, in which there was a massive increase in what you could earn for an ordinary education doing rather ordinary things that didn't really require a lot of skill. It is not sensible for the US and many European countries to send 50 per cent of their children to college, expecting them all to somehow be legislators or managers. That's a hard reality that Europeans and Americans haven't been able to face. They have a lot of unemployment among their own children, and then they import people from the Third World to do the jobs that they won't do.'

Peter Morici, Professor of International Business at Maryland University, quoted by Martin Webber, Business Editor, 24 December 2014

Operations workforces are now being sourced in emerging economies:

'Intel is cutting 1,500 jobs in Costa Rica as it takes steps to cut 5 percent of its workforce by the end of the fiscal year. The job cuts, which will happen over the next two fiscal quarters, are at a site that does chip assembly and testing, said Chuck Mulloy, an Intel spokesman. The assembly and testing operations will be moved to sites in Malaysia, Vietnam and Chengdu, China, where similar functions are already performed.'

Agam Shah, IDG News Service, April 2014

Other pressures, too, are transforming this vital business area:

- big data
- the Internet of Things (IoT)
- new technologies
- globalization.

Big data

In recent years we have experienced, according to Sundar Swaminathan (Senior Director of Industry Strategy and Marketing at Oracle Corporation) writing in 2012, a 'data deluge':

- More than 90 per cent of data in the world today has been created in the last two years, with 80 per cent of it being unstructured, such as images, audio, video, social media, web pages and emails.
- 8 trillion gigabytes of new data were created in 2011.
- Data is expanding at a rate that doubles every two years.
- By 2020 the digital universe will be 40 trillion gigabytes.
- Most US companies have at least 100 terabytes stored.

Businesses are collecting this flood of data via a variety of sources, often in near-real time:

- Electronic On Board Recorders (EOBRs) in trucks
- sensors and radio-frequency identification (RF ID) tags in trailers
- RF readers in distribution centres
- handheld devices (smartphones and tablet PCs)
- business-to-business data exchanges.

To help them process and analyse this data, organizations are introducing new software tools to manage otherwise known as 'big data'.

'[The term "big data"] evolved in 2013–14 and describes the volumes of structured, semi-structured and unstructured

data – often derived from online purchasing information – that can be mined for commercial information. Data analysis has a major impact today on the efficiencies of operations and in logistics and supply chain management, significantly lowering costs and creating major efficiencies in terms of the time and resources required in manufacturing and supply systems. Companies need a strategy to handle the data deluge to acquire, organize and analyze this information. This data can equip executives and operations personnel with whole new insights into their customers, operations, and partner networks, helping them make better strategic and real-time decisions that offer real competitive advantage

Sundar Swaminathan, Oracle's *Profit* magazine

So technology is now centre-stage in logistics, supply chain management and operations management, just as it has permeated every other area of business – and, again, this is resulted in difficulties in recruitment of technically capable staff.

The Internet of Things (IoT)

The Internet of Things as a concept is now beginning to get a lot of attention as a reality – and it will have quite dramatic effects on stock control and supply chain management:

'The Industrial Internet of Things will transform companies and countries, opening up a new era of economic growth and

competitiveness. We see a future where the intersection of people, data and intelligent machines will have far-reaching impacts on the productivity, efficiency and operations of industries around the world.'

Accenture, www.accenture.com

The IoT has come into being as a result of several factors – the ubiquity today of the Internet, low-cost sensors in all fields, from medical diagnostics to location detection, and fast and reliable data transfer rates.

The IoT is becoming a huge connected network, linking computers and the Internet with intelligent sensors and devices in our homes, workplaces and in every part of our lives. This increasingly sophisticated network of systems will bring more convenience, security and efficiencies into our lives, allowing us to do more with less.. These 'smart' embedded devices will permit the automation of many applications that are manually controlled today:

- simple applications for smart thermostat systems and laundry washer-driers using WiFi for remote monitoring
- advanced applications like Smart Grids, including heart-monitoring implants and 'wearable' health-monitoring devices
- biochips for animals
- cars equipped with sensors for many new applications (people, street 'furniture', other cars)
- sensors and controls for security, police, fire, search and rescue operations.

Far more automation will simplify our lives and make them safer.

IoT will have a significant impact on operations management and will be key element of smarter manufacturing. While manufacturing companies have incorporated sensors and computerized automation into manufacturing systems for a long time now, these have often been disconnected from IT and operational systems. IoT overcomes this gap, enabling items in the physical world, and sensors within or attached to these items, to communicate with the Internet via wireless and wired network connections.

The Internet of Things:

- gathers and transmits data from inanimate objects (e.g. industrial equipment, medical devices)
- gathers and transmits data from living objects (e.g. people, animals and even plants)
- share this data with software systems and with people, from factory floor workers to plant managers.

New technologies

New technology, more generally, is revolutionizing manufacturing operations, not only as a means of providing administrative support at lower costs, but directly, as a means of making products. Perhaps the most significant of these new technologies is 3D printing, which is now becoming mainstream.

3D printing

3D printing, or 'additive manufacturing', slowly builds up layers of materials to 'print' solid objects according to a digital blueprint or set of instructions in its memory. A new business has even begun to scan people and create perfect miniature statues of them! Building complex products by adding tiny layer by tiny layer of material, rather than cutting out a shape by machining parts by removing metal, these printers can produce detailed and intricate products that are difficult or expensive to create by other means.

It remains to be seen whether 3D printing will constitute a new 'industrial revolution', as some like to claim, but its impacts certainly look set to be profound.

'The invention or the implementation of the assembly line changed the way manufacturing works and 3D printing is going to change the way manufacturing works in the future. When the web took off, it gave us the tool for everybody ... to become a publisher... Well, with 3D printing, we're all able to be manufacturers.'

Doug Angus-Lee, Rapid Prototype Account Manager, Javelin Technologies, Oakville, Ontario

The list of materials that can be ingested and outputted by 3D printers is growing, some might say into sci-fi territory. The capabilities of 3D printing hardware are evolving rapidly, too. They can build larger components and achieve greater precision and finer resolution at higher speeds and lower costs. Together, these advances have brought the technology to a tipping point – it appears ready to emerge from its niche status and become a viable alternative to conventional manufacturing processes in an increasing number of applications.

Should this happen, the technology would transform manufacturing flexibility – for example, by allowing companies to slash development time, eliminate tooling costs, and simplify production runs – while making it possible to create complex shapes and structures that weren't feasible before. Moreover, additive manufacturing would help companies improve the productivity of materials by eliminating the waste that accrues in traditional (subtractive) manufacturing and would thus spur the formation of a beneficial circular economy.

'The promise of a 3-D printing-based supply chain is simple: Additive manufacturing will democratize the manufacturing process.'

Ed Morris, director of NAMII

78

Globalization

The term 'globalization' in economic or business terms can be applied to three principal phenomena:

1 The integration of national economies as the flow of goods and capital across borders increases
2 The fragmentation of businesses' operations internationally, as they locate each stage of production in the country where it can be done at the least cost. (As we have seen, typically, less skilled activities are sent abroad while more skill-intensive activities are kept at home.)
3 The transmitting of ideas for new products and new ways of making products around the globe.

These have had – and will continue to have – a major impact on organizations' strategies and operations, especially in the liberal economies of the West. In the case of the UK, which has one of the most open economies in the world, these impacts include:

● High levels of foreign direct investment – both inwards and outwards
● Rising levels of import penetration
● A speeding-up of the process by which the comparative advantage of an industry alters over time – largely because of the speedier diffusion of new technology
● Structural change in industries (e.g. long-term reduction in output and employment in industries such as textiles and other manufacturing sectors)
● A reduction in the UK government's ability to levy business taxes freely – because globalized corporations can move production to countries offering the lowest tax base.

Thus for the UK, as throughout the West, these impacts require both businesses and government to:

● improve the skills and flexibility of the workforce, as human capital becomes ever more crucial as a factor determining long-term economic growth
● invest in high-value goods and services (e.g. in high- and medium-high technology manufacturing and in knowledge-intensive service sectors).

MBA recommended reading list

Jay Heizer and Barry Render, *Operations Management: Sustainability and Supply Chain Management*, 11th edition (Pearson, 2013)

Nigel Slack, Alistair Brandon-Jones and Robert Johnston, *Operations Management*, 7th edition (Pearson, 2013)

Summary

The term 'operations' is often used for the corporate area in businesses responsible for the production of goods or services. This includes all activities to create and deliver products or services, from procuring suppliers and materials to logistics and supply chain management.

There are many changes taking place in international business that are impacting on operations management. One powerful force for change is in new technology, which is directly revolutionizing manufacturing operations, not only as a means of providing administrative support at lower costs, but directly, as a means of making products. The Internet, too, is yielding vast amounts of data that can be analysed in 'big data' systems for commercial advantage from greater efficiencies.

As globalization and competitive pressures on organizations increase, new product development (npd) becomes important as a source of competitive advantage.

SUNDAY
MONDAY
TUESDAY
WEDNESDAY
THURSDAY
FRIDAY
SATURDAY

Fact-check (answers at the back)

1. To what does the term 'operations' relate to?
   a) The sales teams' activities in organizations ❏
   b) The corporate area in businesses responsible for the production of goods or services ❏
   c) The ways in which an organization's export strategy is carried out in different countries ❏
   d) It's just another name for 'business activities' ❏

2. Which departments in organizations typically have the greatest concentration of resources, people and assets?
   a) Sales departments ❏
   b) Accounts departments ❏
   c) Human resources departments ❏
   d) Operations departments ❏

3. Why are operations departments frequently viewed as particular sources of competitive advantage?
   a) Because they are low cost ❏
   b) Because they produce the organization's products or services ❏
   c) Because they control the quality of the finished products or services ❏
   d) Because their overtime payments may be cut to allow lower prices ❏

4. What is a significant problem facing operations departments
   a) Recruitment and retention of skilled people ❏
   b) Obtaining raw materials at the necessary cost to drive profits ❏
   c) Trades union activities that cause disruption in production ❏
   d) Controlling production staff's wages and overtime payments ❏

5. What is 'big data'?
   a) Numerical data using more than three decimal places ❏
   b) Numerical data that exceeds the processing power of an organization's IT department ❏
   c) The flood of near real-time data that businesses are collecting through a variety of sources ❏
   d) More data than a conventional PC can hold ❏

6. In what major way is 'big data' affecting operations and logistics in organizations?
a) By equipping executives and operations personnel with whole new insights into their customers, operations and partner networks, particularly for greater efficiencies in logistics and supply chain management ❑
b) By providing justification for more powerful IT systems ❑
c) By assisting the accounts departments to improve costing systems ❑
d) By increasing the need for training in data analysis techniques ❑

7. Where and how will the most dramatic effects of the Internet of Things (IoT) be felt in operations departments?
a) On the speed of the Internet in organizations ❑
b) On stock control and supply chain management systems in organizations ❑
c) On the cost of downloading data from the Internet ❑
d) By the maintenance staff to keep data recording equipment running ❑

8. What does the term 'additive manufacturing' mean?
a) Making more products than had been asked for by forecasting systems ❑
b) Adding the production flows of different manufacturing processes together ❑
c) Another term for '3D printing' ❑
d) Adding more manufacturing lines to an operations department ❑

9. How may the globalization of production affect operations departments in organizations?
a) By lowering the wages of production workers to the lowest levels around the world ❑
b) By raising the incentive to produce in regions with relatively low-cost access to foreign markets ❑
c) By spreading management practices from the West to other, poorer countries ❑
d) By planning production volumes to match shipping capabilities ❑

10. By what is the power of operations, manufacturing, logistics and supply chain management in operations departments today mostly driven? ❑
a) A better-educated workforce ❑
b) Greater fluency in foreign languages under the pressure of globalization ❑
c) The forces of 'technology plus globalization' ❑
d) The costs of staff wages and overtime payments ❑

SUNDAY

MONDAY

TUESDAY

WEDNESDAY

THURSDAY

FRIDAY

SATURDAY

FRIDAY

Organizational behaviour and human resources management

The importance of organizational behaviour and HR departments and their impacts on communications and efficiencies in the management of businesses receive a lot of attention in MBA degrees and in business schools today.

People, processes and work link organizational behaviour (OB) and HR management (HRM), emphasizing intercultural and cross-cultural perspectives for organizational development, talent management, personal development and leadership. Emotional intelligence (EI) is emphasized increasingly in HR departments and executive boardrooms as a useful skill to increase people's abilities to recognize behaviours, moods and impulses, and to manage them effectively in any situation.

The ability to understand people's emotions and how they may be controlled encourages better management and more effective communications in workplaces.

From Theory X to Theory Y ... and beyond

In 1911 the US mechanical engineer Frederick W. Taylor (1856–1915) published his groundbreaking study *Principles of Scientific Management*, in which he addressed the issue of how to motivate workers to produce more. Taylor argued that workers were primarily motivated by money and accordingly developed a differential piece-rate system for the workplace: those workers who did not meet the expected output received a lesser rate of pay, while those who achieved or exceeded the expected output earned the higher rate. This approach has subsequently become known as **Theory X**, and has been much criticized on account of its rather reductive approach to both motivation and human nature.

Strikingly absent from Taylor's understanding of motivation was the role of group behaviour. This was addressed directly by a new generation of theorists (writing from the 1920s until as late as the 1960s), **human relationists**, who argued that, in addition to money, workers sought respect, fair treatment and attention; they wanted to be wanted.

The Hawthorne Experiments

In the 1920s workplace efficiency researchers observed how lighting affected workers assembling electronic components at Western Electric's Hawthorne plant near Chicago. Results indicated that lighting did not affect production consistently – increasing light increased production, but reducing light also increased production! Workers, it seemed, weren't responding to the change in lighting but to the fact that they were being observed by the researchers – later dubbed the 'Hawthorne Effect'. Management was taking an interest in them and that was enough to increase productivity!

Their studies revealed that a worker's motivation was shaped not only by his or her personality and needs but also by the group to which he or she belonged. While one clique of workers might have developed an ethic of hard work and a sense of responsibility, another might encourage 'clock watching' and doing only so much work as was required and no more.

The next generation of theorists focused on the role of the manager in improving efficiency and output. Previously, management had been about control; now it was about facilitation by meeting workers' needs. People work to make a living, of course, but they also work to fulfil certain needs, including:

- to contribute to organizational objectives
- to attain a feeling of accomplishment
- to use their creativity in the work environment.

To maximize motivation, managers need to keep the full variety of needs in mind when dealing with workers. This approach has since been termed **Theory Y**, as it so sharply contrasts with Taylor's.

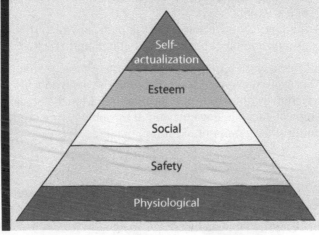

Maslow's hierarchy of needs

The classic tool for understanding employees' varying needs is still Abraham Maslow's 'hierarchy of needs', first outlined in 1943 but given its fullest expression in his book *Motivation and Personality* (1954).

Self-actualization

Esteem

Social

Safety

Physiological

> **Self-actualization** – personal growth and fulfilment
> **Esteem needs** – achievement, status, responsibility, reputation
> **Social** – belonging and affection needs, family, relationships, groups
> **Safety** – protection, stability, order, security
> **Physiological** – biological and basic life needs, air, food, water, warmth

Understanding the particular needs of a particular employee (rather than applying a wholesale theory to a whole team or workforce) is key here.

Self-direction, self-control and effective, two-way communication are all key values in the Theory Y approach.

Most recently of all, theorists have emphasized an all-round, or **'systemic'**, approach to motivation, looking at five main strands or components:

1 the individual – the person in focus
2 the formal organization – in which the person is unquestionably a part
3 the informal organization – the social dimensions to which the individual adheres
4 the fusion process, in which the first three modify and shape one another
5 the physical environment – the place in which the organizational behaviour is exhibited and enacted.

All these work together to determine organizational behaviour. This systemic approach is rooted in the behavioural sciences: psychology (the study of individual behaviour), sociology (the study of social behaviour) and anthropology (the study of the cultural development of human beings).

Organizational behaviour (OB)

Behavioural scientists try to work out why people behave the way they do, both as individuals and in groups. They also investigate the factors that shape personality, including genetic, situational, environmental, cultural and social factors, and analyse personality types, and the relationship between personality traits and the success of a business. Does an authoritarian manager have the effect of getting things done in the face of a crisis or does he or she undermine workers' self-esteem? Generally, experts conclude that a good balance of personality types is useful for an organization but that the more negative aspects of each must be carefully handled. Self-awareness is crucial.

Assessment tools

Personal and personality assessment tools include the Myers-Briggs Type Indicator (MBTI) and the DISC system. DISC is easier to understand and apply than MBTI, less clinical and more memorable for those being assessed.

Researchers have also developed a number of concepts that show how workplace interpersonal relationships can become warped and have a negative impact on business. These include:

- **Stereotyping** – the process of categorizing people based on partial or limited information
- **Halo effect** – the use of known personal traits as the basis for an overall evaluation
- **Projection** – an individual's attribution of his or her own undesirable traits or characteristics to others
- **Groupthink** (see Tuesday).

What is a group?

Perhaps the most basic issue scholars have addressed in the area of group behaviour is the definition of 'group'. They have agreed that there is no one definition. Therefore, they have looked more at why people join groups, types of groups, and group activities and goals. Studies have focused on group norms, individuals' behaviour within groups and how it changes, their roles within groups, and what groups can accomplish that individuals can not. Many researchers believe that a

SUNDAY
MONDAY
TUESDAY
WEDNESDAY
THURSDAY
FRIDAY
SATURDAY

> group is more than the sum of the individual members, even though its goals, interactions and performance are determined primarily by the individuals within it.

Many researchers have suggested ways in which organizations can recast or restructure workplace relationships in order to stimulate maximum job satisfaction and hence productivity. Studies have sought to identify those company cultures that lead to better communication, increased engagement, a reduction in stress, and a better quality of life among employees.

Quality circles – in which teams drawn from every area of a company identify and resolve work-related problems – and **participative management schemes,** in which employees are encouraged to offer, comment on and implement new ideas in the workplace – are two widespread practical models that have arisen from such research.

Theory Z

The US organizational behaviour scientist William Ouchi (1943–) recommends that companies look to Japanese management concepts to enrich management practices. This he dubbed 'Theory Z'. Ouchi believes that using Theory Z reduces employee turnover, increases work commitment, improved morale and job satisfaction and greatly increases productivity. He proposes that organizations should:

- develop strong company philosophies and culture
- set up staff development programmes and long-term employment policies to encourage loyalty
- have policies for consensus in decision-making
- encourage employees to be 'generalists' (but with some specializations!)
- show a sincere concern for the happiness and well-being of workers
- have informal management controls in places but alongside formalized assessment measures
- recognize individuals' responsibilities but within the context of a team.

Of course, not all such ideas will be appropriate for every organization. If there is one thing that all researchers have recognized, it is that every company is different, with its own 'personality' and needs.

Key issues in organizational behaviour

Teamwork and collaboration

Many organizations include 'teamwork' and 'collaboration' prominently among their stated values, but what it is that makes people work together well, and, conversely, what can cause collaboration to break down? As we might expect, there is no catch-all answer, but communication styles seem to be crucial.

In modern business, email has become perhaps the primary tool for efficient, speedy and cheap communications. However, there is growing evidence that email, like other 'mechanical' forms of communication, undermines effective collaboration by fostering feelings of mistrust and remoteness. By contrast, face-to-face discussion – although possibly time-consuming – appears to improve teamwork.

Good leadership is vital in fostering effective teamwork.

Leadership vs. management

Organizational behaviour scientists have drawn attention to the important and useful distinction between leadership and management:

- **Management** is the process of accomplishing tasks
- **Leadership** is the process of getting things done by influencing other people.

A good manager is not necessarily a good leader, and vice versa.

There are common characteristics shared by leaders – intelligence, dependability and responsibility among them – but otherwise it is hard to pin down exactly what qualities are needed and whether these can be learned or acquired.

Communication

Good, clear and timely communications are critical to the efficient running of any business. The following 'soft skills' are crucial:

- an ability to **listen attentively** to the other party – customers, employees, managers, peers...
- an ability to **orchestrate discussion**
- an ability to **negotiate** with the goal of achieving a win/win outcome.

It is important that the links between effective communications in businesses and types of organizational behaviour are recognized.

> *'One lesson from OB is informal communications can be even more important than formal organizational communications. Employees often obtain more information from their direct managers – and even from their co-workers informally through the grapevine — than they do from formal organizational announcements.'*
>
> Brian Kreissl, blog on 'HR Policies and Practice' in the
> *Canadian HR Reporter*, 2011

Power and conflict

According to organizational behaviour scientists, there are five basic types of power that managers and leaders use to influence subordinates. The table shows the advantages and disadvantages of each:

Power type	Definition	Advantage	Disadvantage
Reward	The extent to which managers may use rewards to influence others	Produces quick and easy wins	May tempt unethical behaviour to meet targets

Coercive	The opposite of reward power, used by managers to punish subordinates	Leads to short-term and quick obedience (e.g. in the armed forces)	In the long-term, if wielded unintelligently, produces dysfunctional behaviour
Legitimate	Power and authority derived from the manager's position in the organization	Power that is owned by right and easy to deploy	Workers may not feel a sense of commitment or are unwilling to co-operate
Referent	Derives from employees' respect for a manager and wish to emulate that manager	Can be a simple spin-off from good leadership	Difficult to apply in cross-cultural situations and relies on trust
Expert	Derives from respect for an individual's high level of knowledge or highly specialized skills	The superior may not rank higher, formally, than the other people	Expertise diminishes as knowledge is shared

Inexperienced managers often use political tactics to exert influence over others, using stratagems such as:

● blaming others for their own mistakes
● forming 'power coalitions' and 'power bases'
● flattering colleagues who appear to be useful as allies
● using overly threatening behaviour
● developing alliances in subordinates for support.

Unfortunately, such tactics often lead to conflict, another area that is much studied by organizational behaviour scientists.

In any workplace, conflict – both at the individual and group level – is inevitable. The problem is how to deal with such conflict effectively and efficiently, and even to harness it constructively. Solutions might include fostering:

● **mutual problem** solving involving subordinates and peers so as to build trust in teams
● **compromise** – this is not always a good idea but flexibility will overcome barriers

- **avoidance** – if issues and conflicts can be avoided, then do so (though some issues need to be faced down!)
- **displaying honesty and integrity** – this will pay off in the longer-term.

All too often, however – researchers have discovered – conflict resolutions are only temporary and they have sought ways to make them more permanent in order to build or to reinforce positions of authority – often mistakenly!

Managing change

Change management is another major area of OB research, and has become crucial as organizations struggle to adapt and evolve in the face of social and demographic trends, new technologies, economic cycles and regulation, among other things. Key questions include:

- How does change affect people in an organization?
- How can change be managed to maximize its success and minimize unintended disruptions?
- Do we agree on the need for change?

OB scientists distinguish between first-order change – change that is incremental and ongoing – and second-order change – change that is radical and episodic. Both can be disruptive if not handled carefully, but second-order change requires a very safe and skilful pair of hands indeed.

Downsizing

Downsizing is perhaps one of the most potentially disruptive second-order changes a company can undertake and demands skilful and sensitive change management if it is to be successful. Downsizing affects not only those workers who are laid off but, crucially for the organization, those who remain, who may easily become demoralized, disengaged and mistrustful if they perceive that managers have acted in a high-handed or unfair way. Handled well, however, the remaining workforce can 'rally to the cause', working harder and more collaboratively and in other ways that will ultimately benefit the organization.

Emotional intelligence

Good communications in the workplace are affected by levels of emotional intelligence (EI) demonstrated by staff at all levels in a business. The part played by EI in effective communications and better management practices is increasingly being recognized today. The following quote is indicative in this respect:

'A bright future belongs to those organizations where positive, adaptive, purposeful and empathetic relationships define the quality of care of those they serve. Liberty Lutheran, Ambler, PA [a not-for-profit company that runs hospices], considers staff its most important resource. We continually source and develop dynamic business tools that support our commitment to providing world-class internal customer service to realize a competitive benefit. A well-cared-for staff will not only stay, but will fully

97

engage in the process of nurturing meaningful professional relationships amongst one another and especially, our residents and family members.

We've worked to create a culture defined by open communication, trust and accountability...'

Christopher Ridenhour, for Liberty Lutheran, 'Bringing Emotional Intelligence to Staff Training', *Leading Age Magazine* (March/April 2014)

The concept of emotional intelligence is hardly new, but it was only in the 1990s that it became the subject of serious academic research. Two of its pioneering theorists, US psychologists John D. Mayer and Peter Salovey, defined it as 'the subset of social intelligence that involves the ability to monitor one's own and others' feelings and emotions, to discriminate among them and to use this information to guide one's thinking and actions'. Another key theorist was Daniel Goleman, whose seminal work *Emotional Intelligence: Why It Can Matter More Than IQ* (1995) continues to dominate this field today.

EI allows difficult and sensitive situations in the workplace to be resolved more readily and satisfactorily for the longer term.

'The willingness to admit your weaknesses and your vulnerabilities is actually very powerful. You can gain strength by admitting your faults to yourself and your peers. When you admit it, you make it a part of what we share as information about ourselves. It makes it okay for me to bring it up, which is crucial for working through conflict. You can even joke about it to ease tension. "You're doing that thing again."'

Daniel Goleman, 'Finding Strength in Admitting Your Weakness', March 2015

MBA recommended reading list

Travis Bradberry, *Emotional Intelligence 2.0* (TalentSmart, 2009)

Jill Dann, *Emotional Intelligence In A Week* (John Murray Learning, 2016)

Daniel Goleman, *Emotional Intelligence: Why It Can Matter More Than IQ* (Bloomsbury, 1996)

Daniel Goleman, *Working with Emotional Intelligence* (Bloomsbury, 1999)

Laurie J. Mullins, *Management and Organisational Behaviour* (FT Publishing International, 2013)

Summary

Organizational behavioural studies in areas such as individual behaviours, group behaviours, organizational structures, and organizational processes help to describe and predict how workers will behave in organized environments. They investigate motivation and job satisfaction in organizations in order to understand the relationship between motivation, reward and improved productivity in the workplace.

Change and conflict management and emotional intelligence are critical subjects in today's human resource departments, and indeed in every part and at every level of organizations. Emotional intelligence, for example, assists the management of people by encouraging managers' abilities to recognize behaviours, moods and impulses and to manage people effectively in any situation.

The ability to understand people's emotions and how they may be controlled encourages better management and more effective communications in workplaces.

SUNDAY
MONDAY
TUESDAY
WEDNESDAY
THURSDAY
FRIDAY
SATURDAY

Fact-check (answers at the back)

1. What is 'organizational behaviour'?
   a) The study of how to control teams of workers ❑
   b) The encouragement of better manners in working groups ❑
   c) An academic discipline that describes and predicts workers' behaviours in organized group environments ❑
   d) The study of how to get the most from working in groups ❑

2. What are the formal links between studies in 'organizational behaviour' and the discipline of HR management
   a) Legally – by laws ❑
   b) By people, processes and work ❑
   c) By trades unions' rules ❑
   d) Because understanding behaviours encourages better working practices ❑

3. In which decade did emotional intelligence (EI) finally gain prominence and recognition in management studies?
   a) In the 1930s ❑
   b) In the 1950s ❑
   c) In the 1970s ❑
   d) In the 1990s ❑

4. What was the breakthrough idea of F.W. Taylor concerning workers' motivation and productivity?
   a) The creation of team leaders ❑
   b) The introduction of trades unions' shop stewards ❑
   c) To use systems of planning and rewards to increase workers' levels of motivation and productivity ❑
   d) The suggestion that only more money works effectively as a workplace reward ❑

5. What or who are 'human relationists'?
   a) People whose ideas on workers' levels of motivation include giving workers more personal and individual attention ❑
   b) Scientists who try to find relational links between workers ❑
   c) HR staff who specialize in tracking down family relationships in organizations ❑
   d) People who recommend employing relatives in businesses ❑

6. What were the 'Hawthorne Experiments'?
a) Experiments in horticulture in the workplace ❏
b) Experiments designed to show how workers' performances are affected by changes to working environments ❏
c) Attempts to create productivity efficiencies for their own sake ❏
d) Psychological experiments designed to achieve improvements to working efficiencies ❏

7. What are 'quality circles'?
a) Groups of workers taking tea breaks in their working areas ❏
b) Circles of workers formed by managers to speak to them in their workplaces ❏
c) Team-based approaches to identifying and resolving work-related problems ❏
d) Games to encourage fitness and to relieve boredom in the workplace ❏

8. What is the 'halo effect'?
a) An award for good operations management ❏
b) An award for the best workers ❏
c) A form of cognitive bias in which an impression of a someone or thing is skewed by their appearance or the environment around them to give a false impression ❏
d) How someone with an extrovert personality can rise in management circles ❏

9. How do behavioural scientists differentiate between managers and leaders?
a) Managers discipline workers but leaders only reward them ❏
b) Managers complete tasks through people but leaders inspire and influence people to achieve ❏
c) Leaders are not usually visible to workers but managers are constantly seen in the workplace ❏
d) Leaders are paid more than managers ❏

10. Why should emotional intelligence be fostered in the workplace?
a) To gain information about workers' private lives ❏
b) To allow individuals to monitor their own and others' feelings and emotions to better guide their decisions, activities and communications ❏
c) To prevent or reduce the likelihood of emotions getting out of control in the workplace ❏
d) To help workers become more intelligent ❏

SATURDAY

Research and change management

By a combination of sensitively applied quantitative and qualitative research conducted with an organization's employees, management, suppliers, customers – both past and present – and all key stakeholders, a clear understanding of where the business is today can be obtained as a solid foundation from which to determine the change-management process for the future.

Research programmes form critical elements of change-management processes for people and for organizations. Research is the vital first step to understand how people are behaving today, why and how they feel about their work and its objectives – and then how they might react to change to new working directions and methods.

Rooted in that research, change management – a vital component of all MBA programmes – tries to realign people and organizations to perform more effectively by working in new ways.

Using research

Both quantitative and qualitative research are commonly used in management consulting to provide an initial, reliable picture of an organization's situation. By using one or, preferably, both of these research methods, a consultant can then begin to form opinions about the best ways to effect change, to achieve a much-improved future position for that organization.

Quantitative research

Quantitative research relies primarily on numerical data as the main subject of analysis. Its most typical tool is the **questionnaire survey**, which uses a series of closed questions to gather large quantities of data from a wide number of people, the results of which can then be analysed by computer. Questionnaires can be handed out and then collected face to face, sent by post or, as is becoming increasingly common, posted online.

Generally speaking, however, the more personal the contact between the researcher and the potential respondent, the higher the response rate. Thus, online surveys have a response rate of less than 20 per cent, while for face-to-face surveys this figure is usually a great deal higher.

Primarily, quantitative research is used because it is statistically more valid and thus more reliable and objective and often reduces and restructures a complex problem to a more limited number of variables. Under controlled circumstances, it can be used to test theories and hypotheses and establish cause and effect, thus providing important information for business decisions. However, it is less detailed than qualitative research data and a desired, particular response from the participant may be missed.

Qualitative research

Typically, qualitative research provides much more in-depth information about people's reactions, feelings, perceptions and decision-making processes. It relies on words rather than numerical data. The classical instrument of qualitative research is the **focus group**, although the **one-to-one interview** is also common. The results of qualitative research, based on a relatively small group, are used to represent the whole demographic being researched.

Because qualitative research is extremely labour-intensive, it tends to be small scale. Focus groups require highly trained conveners, responses and interviews need to be transcribed, and the results analysed by researchers, ideally different from those who conducted the focus group or interview. Nonetheless, the ultimate result of qualitative research is incomparably richer and more meaningful.

Qualitative research is used typically in circumstances in which valuable data for the design of a new product or service is required, including subjective information on behaviour patterns and users' needs. It can provide subjective information on emotions and personality characteristics that quantitative studies cannot achieve and a variety of information essential to design a product or service to fit into users' lives.

In summary:

Research methods	Advantages	Disadvantages
Quantitative	• Statistical data from large samples • More reliable • Yields important information for business decisions	• Less detailed than qualitative research data • A desired, particular response may be missed
Qualitative	• Provides subjective information on behaviour patterns and users' needs • Gathers essential information to design a new product or service to fit into users' lives	• Does not have a valid statistical base • Results may be skewed by interviewer's bias • The constituents in the sample must be chosen very carefully

Triangulation

Triangulation is the term for where a number of research methods are used to investigate an issue. For example, to study the effect of a proposed closure of a factory site on its staff you could use a combination of some or all of the following:

- questionnaire survey of all staff, carried out face-to-face
- in-depth interviews with sample groups of staff at different levels
- focus-group discussions to which all staff are invited
- an analysis of personnel data covering sickness, absence, etc.

The potential result of such multidimensional research would be to provide the company with the richest possible understanding of how it might best carry out the planned closure with minimal impact on staff – an extreme example of change management, the area to which we will now turn.

Change management

The subject of change management is much used in management consulting. In simple terms, it means understanding:

- where an organization is today
- where it wants to be in the future
- how to move it most effectively to where it should be by changing organizational procedures and behaviours and also those of individuals.

In 1996 the Harvard professor John Kotter published the best-selling *Leading Change* – a seminal study of change management.

John Kotter

Dr John P. Kotter is widely regarded as the foremost writer, speaker and authority on the subjects of leadership and change management – how the best organizations achieve successful change. As Harvard Business School's Konosuke Matsushita Professor of Leadership, Emeritus, Kotter's intellectual dominance of successful change management and leadership are well proven. He created and co-founded Kotter International, helping Global 5000 company leaders to lead change in complex and large-scale businesses.

Since then hundreds of articles and books have been published on the subject and most have agreed on what constitutes the building blocks of a successful programme. There must be:

1 a **compelling story** – employees must see the point of the change and agree with it
2 **role modelling** – employees must also see the CEO and managers adopting the new desired behaviour.
3 **reinforcing mechanisms** – systems, processes and incentives must align with the new behaviour.
4 **capability building** – employees must acquire the skills needed to make the desired changes.

For all that change management plays a central role in business, and for all that it has become a subject of study in almost every leading MBA course, it is still all too often poorly conducted. In *Leading Change*, back in 1996, Dr Kotter pointed out that only 30 per cent of change programmes succeeded; more than a decade later, in 2008, a McKinsey survey of 3,199 executives around the world found that the success rate was just the same – one in three. Clearly, much more work needs to be done.

One diagnosis of this problem is that, while the four principles outlined above are clearly common sense, the managers who implement them all too often fail to take into account the realities of human nature, which is not always rational. Individuals' behaviours are deeply entrenched and changing them – *permanently* – is challenging.

> *'Leaders must understand and apply the knowledge of behavioural psychology to manage organizational change successfully. In the past, efforts at organizational change have systematically failed because they have neglected the reality that change doesn't happen without individual people changing their thinking, beliefs, and behaviour. In the article by Emily Lawson and Colin Price they argue that change management success, in large organizations, depends on groups and individuals changing the way they function... In effect, management must alter the mind-sets of their employees – no easy task.'*
> Ray Williams, 'Why Change Management Fails in Organizations'

There is also evidence to suggest that managers all too often assume that employees are motivated only by money (see Friday) and use this to underpin their change management programmes.

David Rock, a leadership consultant and author of *Quiet Leadership: Six Steps to Transforming Leadership at Work*, and Jeffrey Schwartz, a research scientist at UCLA, apply neuroscience concepts to leadership and have coined the term 'neuroleadership':

> *'The traditional command-and-control style of management doesn't lead to permanent changes in behavior. Ordering people to change and them telling them how to do it fires the prefrontal cortex's hair trigger connection to the amygdala. The more you try to convince people that you're right and they're wrong, the more they push back. The brain will try to defend itself from threats.'*
>
> David Rock and Jeffrey Shwartz, 'The Neuroscience of Leadership', in *Strategy + Business* (2006)

Case study: Accenture's 'journey management'

Although really focused on large change programmes involving information technology, Accenture, one of the world's leading organizations providing management consulting, technology and outsourcing services, has a concept of 'journey management', developed in 2013, which has wide and general implications for all forms of organizational change. For Accenture, a typical 'journey of change' should be managed in five phases:

1 Assess the current environment and drivers for change – a detailed and fact-based assessment of the current state leads to a deeper understanding of why change needs to be undertaken.

2 Articulate a compelling description of the future state and vision of the organization – leaders responsible for managing a change journey should agree on what the future state of the organization will be – with tangible business outcomes.

3 Assess the gap between current and desired future state – assessments of the functions affected by the change journey, effectiveness of existing talent strategies, relevance of current leadership development programmes, the culture of the organization and more.

4 Create a journey road map to plan and prioritize activities – detail multiple initiatives within the change portfolio and integration points, and prioritize them according to impact and ability of the organization to absorb the changes.

5 Proactively monitor the journey and change portfolio to keep the organization on track – move beyond traditional program management so that multiple strands of work can be coordinated effectively.

It is worth emphasizing here that Accenture's journey begins with a careful, in-depth assessment of 'why change needs to be undertaken' and takes us back to the research methodology with which we began this chapter – the application of good research techniques reduces the likelihood of failure in change management projects right from the outset.

Flexibility

Flexibility is critical in the implementation of research results because there is always the temptation to delay putting recommendations into practice until there is very clear evidence that it will be successful. The champion of the research project will usually bear the responsibility for any failures! So pragmatism and flexibility in the interpretation and implementation of results in often critical to success.

MBA recommended reading list

Mike Bourne and Pippa Bourne, *Change Management In A Week* (John Murray Learning, 2016)

Esther Cameron and Mike Green, *Making Sense of Change Management: A Complete Guide to the Models, Tools and Techniques of Organizational Change* (Kogan Page, 2015)

John P. Kotter, *Leading Change*, new edition (Harvard Business Review Press, 2012)

Michael D. Myers, *Qualitative Research in Business and Management*, 2nd edition (SAGE Publications, 2013)

Richard Smith et al. (eds), *The Effective Change Manager's Handbook: Essential Guidance to the Change Management Body of Knowledge* (Kogan Page, 2014)

Summary

By the careful and thoughtful application of suitable research techniques, managers can achieve a clear understanding of where the business is today as a solid foundation for a new future. The changes required can be defined for the organization's management in the consultants' report but the actual changes required, over time, take a lot of management attention and constant effort to keep the implementation of those changes on track. Qualitative and quantitative research techniques may show the way but the hardest tasks often lie in the determined implementation of the changes, while allowing for a degree of flexibility as unexpected roadblocks occur.

SUNDAY
MONDAY
TUESDAY
WEDNESDAY
THURSDAY
FRIDAY
SATURDAY

Fact-check (answers at the back)

1. **What is quantitative research?**
   a) Research conducted in quantum physics ❑
   b) Research conducted with a numerically large sample base ❑
   c) Research conducted in small quantities ❑
   d) Research by quantity surveyors ❑

2. **What is qualitative research?**
   a) Finding out how suitable job applicants are ❑
   b) Small individual or group discussions to discover how people react to certain, often complex, situations and subjects ❑
   c) Trying to understand how quality control systems work best ❑
   d) Marketing research into what drives quality in brands ❑

3. **What are focus groups?**
   a) Study groups used to help short-sighted people to read better ❑
   b) Workplace groups set up to advise management on problems on which to focus ❑
   c) A research method commonly used in qualitative research ❑
   d) Groups of people with a common interest or background ❑

4. **Why does qualitative research tend to be small scale?**
   a) Because it uses only a few people in its implementation ❑
   b) Because the use of too many people obscures the results ❑
   c) Because it is hugely labour-intensive ❑
   d) Because it is conducted using discussions in controllable groups ❑

5. **What does the term 'triangulation' mean in research terms?**
   a) Using just three groups of people in the research programme ❑
   b) Bringing a number of research methods to bear upon a question ❑
   c) A simple research technique that uses just three main questions ❑
   d) Checking the research results at least three times ❑

6. **What is change management?**
   a) An employee recruitment technique ❑
   b) A strategy to deliberately confuse competitors by suddenly changing business direction ❑
   c) Managing a longer-term change for an organization to a new defined future ❑
   d) Recruiting a new management team to replace those currently in place ❑

7. Change management is best achieved by which of the following?
a) Authoritarian management ❑
b) Understanding where an organization is today, where it wants to be, and how to move it most effectively to where it should be in the future ❑
c) Issuing new procedures in writing to all employees ❑
d) Inviting the trades unions in the workplace to create change ❑

8. John Kotter's seminal work on change programmes found that...
a) 85 per cent of change management programmes succeed ❑
b) 30 per cent of change programmes fail ❑
c) Change programmes never succeed for very long ❑
d) 30 per cent of change programmes succeed ❑

9. The principal successful motivation in changing employees' behaviours has been shown to be...
a) Financial rewards ❑
b) Paid vacations ❑
c) A diversity of factors including a personal interest in their jobs and a good working environment ❑
d) Threats to workers' employment contracts ❑

10. How is organizational change effected?
a) By changing organizational procedures and behaviours and also those of individuals ❑
b) Only with the support of the trades unions ❑
c) Only over a very long period of time ❑
d) By the use of firm managerial authority ❑

7 × 7

Seven key ideas

1 Limited liability – this concept, intended to protect either creditors or investors, is crucial to much company law.

2 Chief financial officers today grasp advantage and lead growth in conditions of increasing volatility and uncertainty in the global economy by implementing research and strategic planning.

3 Ethics and morals in business life help make the best decisions for the longer term in fast-moving and complex entrepreneurial environments.

4 Strategic planning, allied with marketing, is concerned with the overall direction of the business, making decisions about production and operations, finance, human resources and all business issues.

5 Increased competitive advantage can be gained by giving customers more options and power in commercial engagements, as Internet trading has proved.

6 Emotional intelligence (EI) encourages better management and more effective communications in workplaces.

7 Professionally applied change-management processes move organizations quickly and effectively towards better futures.

Seven resources

1 Keep daily tabs on the forces acting on the world and business at the BBC website: www.bbc.co.uk/news/business

2 Maintain an up-to-date understanding of global economies and their pressures and challenges by subscribing to *The Economist*: www.economist.com/

3 A good guide to how and why businesses should follow ethical principles is 'Business Ethics and Social Responsibility' from the Free Management Library: managementhelp.org/businessethics/index.htm

4 A world-leading resource on marketing management and strategic planning is the Chartered Management Institute's research page: http://www.managers.org.uk/insights/research

5 A key resource on the critical relationships between customers, marketing and operations management is provided by the Institute of Operations Management at: www.iomnet.org.uk/

6 The Chartered Institute of Personnel and Development carries out research for effective communications: www.cipd.co.uk/research/

7 Quantitative and qualitative research techniques are explored further by the Department of Sociology at the University of Warwick (UK): www2.warwick.ac.uk/fac/soc/sociology/staff/academicstaff/hughes/researchprocess/

Seven great companies

1 Amazon is a paradox: a company known for making virtually no profits despite strong revenues and a sizeable market share. CEO Jeff Bezos is now betting on a new technological trend – the Internet of Things – as the next big thing as Amazon continues to ride global pressures, shifts and trends.

2 Ernst & Young Global Limited (EY) is the world's 'most globally integrated professional services organization'. Its motto, 'When business works better, the world works better', should be on the desk of every CEO.

3 Coca-Cola provides a good example of a global organization's approach to corporate responsibility and business ethics: www.coca-colacompany.com/our-company/governance-ethics/governance-ethics

4 Dyson, a great engineering and strategic company, has set a leading example in championing engineering education systems in the UK: www.careers.dyson.com/

5 Apple's new product development process always starts with design and continues into its 'Apple New Product Process' that ensures the right product emerges at the right time.

6 Intel's 'Materials Communications Strategy' delivers communications that are timely, accurate and effective.

7 British Airways (BA) was failing customers and shareholders but introduced a change-management process for the future and is today a well-managed and successful company.

Seven inspiring people

1 Lee Kwan Yew (1923–2015), the founding father of independent Singapore, inspired even China's leaders to manage their citizens in new ways in times of dramatic social and political change

2 Tim Cook (1960–), Apple's CEO, has put his own imprint on the company, with his own set of values and priorities, showing inspiring leadership.

3 Mahatma Gandhi (1869–38), the inspiring leader who fought for the independence of India, believed that life could not be compartmentalized and that all actions are interrelated. A good lesson for business.

4 H. Igor Ansoff (1918–2002), 'the father of strategic management', was a Russian-American applied mathematician and business manager, perhaps best known by marketing and MBA students for his 'Product–Market Growth Matrix'.

5 Carolyn McCall (1961–) joined EasyJet as CEO in 2010 and led the company to record performances and was awarded an OBE for inspirational services to women in business.

6 Michelle Obama (1964–) is an inspirational communicator and uses emotional intelligence to appear confident, likeable and authentic.

7 The UK's Royal Mail is a must-cover case study for MBA business students. CEO Moya Greene (1954–) was named as Financial Times Person of the Year in 2014 and is an inspirational leader managing change in a large organization.

Seven great quotes on change

1 'Business is like a man rowing a boat upstream. He has no choice; he must go ahead or he will go back.' Lewis E. Pierson

2 'Only the wisest and stupidest of men never change.' Confucius

3 'There is nothing more difficult to take in hand, more perilous to conduct, or more uncertain in its success, than to take the lead in the introduction of a new order of things.' Niccolò Machiavelli, *The Prince* (1532)

4 'The rate of change is not going to slow down anytime soon. If anything, competition in most industries will probably speed up even more in the next few decades.' John P. Kotter in *Leading Change* (1996)

5 'We would rather be ruined than changed,
We would rather die in our dread
Than climb the cross of the moment
And let our illusions die.'

W.H. Auden, *The Age of Anxiety: A Baroque Eclogue* (1947)

6 'Everybody has accepted by now that change is unavoidable. But that still implies that change is like death and taxes – it should be postponed as long as possible and no change would be vastly preferable. But in a period of upheaval, such as the one we are living in, change is the norm.' Peter Drucker in *Management Challenges for the 21st Century* (1999)

7 'It's not the progress I mind, it's the change I don't like.'
Mark Twain

Seven top executive MBA courses 2015 (according to *The Economist*)

1 IE Business School, Spain

2 University of Oxford, Saïd Business School, UK

3 Northwestern University, Kellogg School of Management, USA

4 UCLA/NUS Business School, USA/Singapore

5 Northwestern (Kellogg) / York (Schulich), USA/Canada

6 Northwestern (Kellogg) / WHU (Beisheim), USA/Germany

7 Thunderbird School of Global Management, USA

Seven trends for tomorrow

1 New investment trends such as crowd-funding are bringing new innovations to markets faster...

2 The emergence of China and India as global powers will reshape the world and everyone's lives...

3 Augmented Virtual Reality and the 'Internet of Things' will affect future employment...

4 Cyber security and crime-related technology are limiting the exchange of knowledge...

5 New materials will create great changes in transportation and energy use...

6 Global greenhouse gas emissions may have peaked (Energy World, April 2015) – can we relax?

7 Disadvantaged young men in the rich world are falling behind in jobs, social lives and relationships...